JUMP YOUR SHADOW

Jump Your Shadow

Doing Brave Things in a Broken World

Phil Johnson, Ph.D.

Global Next Publishing

Jump Your Shadow: Doing Brave Things in a Broken World.

Edited by JoEllen Smith

Cover design Ali Majoka
grafikali.seven@facebook.com

Contact information:
Global Next Publishing
PO Box 2215
Frisco, Texas 35034
214.733.6577
www.globalnext.org
info@globalnext.org

Dedication

To all those who have jumped for something bigger than themselves.

TABLE OF CONTENTS

INTRODUCTION 9

CHAPTER ONE:
WHY BOTHER JUMPING? 21
Seeing opportunities in a broken world

CHAPTER TWO:
FEAR AND INTELLIGENCE 35
Why smart people are afraid to jump

CHAPTER THREE:
QUESTIONS AND JUMPERS 49
Know the players

CHAPTER FOUR:
JUMPING YOUR SHADOW 61
Choosing to live a big life

CHAPTER FIVE:
MOTIVATIONAL FORCES 79
What makes you jump?

CHAPTER SIX:
YOUR JUMP TEAM 95
Choosing the right people

CHAPTER SEVEN:
DREAMING THROUGH THE FINISH 115
How to dream and get the job done

CHAPTER EIGHT:
JUMP HEROES 135
People who jumped big

CHAPTER NINE:
THE REBOUND 151
Getting up after falling

CHAPTER TEN:
THE ARTICLES.. 165
Evidence of a jump

BIBLIOGRAPHY 329

**Postcards that appear in this book are part of a postcard project in which students participate on Global Next's international leadership conferences. Students are asked to respond to a variety of topics as they relate to our conference themes. I hope you enjoy this small sample of the meaning students have found in the corners of a broken world.*

INTRODUCTION

INTRODUCTION

It was 2:30 am when I landed in Sana'a, the capital of Yemen. I was looking for my contact, Ameen Abdullah. I'd never met him in person, but we had corresponded online and he had agreed to help me in my work: specifically helping to arrange a meeting with Nasser al-Bahri, the former bodyguard and chief of security for Osama bin Laden. Al-Bahri had just published a book in France about his life with the world's most wanted man and his own journey into and out of jihad. I wanted to meet him and talk to him about his life, his notorious associate and his own journey.

Ameen spotted me immediately when I walked through the arrivals door of the airport - which I'm guessing wasn't too hard, since I was the only white guy around. As we got into a taxi together, Ameen turned to me and said, "I never asked you, what made you pick me to help you with this and why exactly are you here to meet this guy? Don't you know this is dangerous?"

What *was* I doing here? Why was I getting into a car with a guy I had never met in a country that had become the new breeding ground for al-Qaeda, infamous for kidnapping Americans and who had recently bombed oil pipelines and power lines leaving the city without electricity during parts of the day and in complete darkness during the night.

To understand why I was in Yemen, you have to understand what I do. I run a small company called Global Next. It's a research group and leadership institute. We track leadership trends, interpersonal relationships issues, cultural shifts and geopolitical trends. And then that information is used in our international conferences where we try to help people connect a few dots, understand the world in context and recognize their purpose in this world. And I suppose this is what brought me to Yemen. Chasing another story about another interesting individual that I hoped would yield some insight into our ever-changing world.

Stories fascinate me. Everyone loves a good story. Stories have the power to teach, to inspire and to move us to action. The world is filled with them and yet so many people are scared to live out the story that God has for their life. But the idea of being part of God's unfolding story in this world can be very compelling. If you're willing to live it. If you're willing to accept the inevitable conflict that exists in any great story. If you're willing to jump your shadow to chase after it.

I think author Donald Miller (2010) had it right when he said, "Somehow we realize that great stories are told in conflict, but we are unwilling to embrace the potential greatness of the story we are actually in. We think God is unjust, rather than a master storyteller." He goes on to say that, "Without story, experiences are just random." And I agree with that. Without recognizing God's unfolding story, all choices, current events, wars, conflicts and personal struggles are indeed just random experiences. They are just noise. It's when you understand those events in the context of a story that they take on meaning.

Any interesting life will have conflict. Any worthwhile existence will have its difficult moments. But we are often obsessed with the pursuit of things that are easy - easy friendships, trouble-free jobs, simple class assignments, and effortless dreams. Most of us would be delighted to have our own private "easy button" to press when things get hard. But easy doesn't make a great story. Easy doesn't change lives or communities. The most meaningful things in life take effort and risk – and they definitely require jumping a few shadows.

To "jump your shadow" is to get out of your comfort zone, figure out how to achieve your dreams and then shape your world. Whether you want to raise money to bring education to forgotten parts of the world, or build an orphanage, or feed the hungry, or start a business or just improve your relationships with your family and friends, you're going to have to take some risks. You’re going to have to jump.

In my book, *The Leadership Paradox,* I shared a story about my friend Paul who lives in Germany. Paul is a great guy. He’s the kind of guy that everyone likes and everyone wants to be around. He was built for impacting others. But Paul doesn’t like to take risks, especially risks that involve people or doing things out of his comfort zone. When I ask Paul about doing difficult things, and reaching out to others in need, he told me that in German, there’s a famous saying that describes the way he feels: *"Er hat angst über seinen schatten zu springen"* In English, it means, “I’m afraid to jump my shadow.” As Paul puts it, he knows it’s just a shadow, but he can’t get past it. And because he can’t get past it, his story is diminished, nothing changes and no one is profoundly impacted.

I think we’ve all felt that way before. We’ve all had things that we were afraid to get past, things, that if we could get past them would distinguish an ordinary life from an extraordinary life. And I’m not necessarily talking only about big and bold actions. Just because someone does daring or outrageous things, doesn’t necessarily mean he’s jumped his shadow. If it’s easy for you, it’s not a shadow to get past. For some people, slowing down, taking time for people or nurturing a relationship are much more difficult than jumping out of an airplane or starting a company.

We all have things to get past. Fears, insecurities, inhibitions, diminished visions, shattered dreams, laziness, selfishness – the list could go on. But I don't want to make you feel too bad about yourself before I give you hope and some suggestions on how to jump your shadow and to have a life that is not only more interesting, more full and more enjoyable, but exponentially more beneficial for the broken world around you.

This book is all about understanding the world in which we're living and how each of us can get past those things that keep us from reaching our potential, living out the stories of our lives and impacting a broken world. Throughout this book I'll share a little of what I've learned along my life of jumping and we'll also take a look at issues like what really motivates us, our selective attention to the opportunities that surround us and how we think about making choices. We'll also look at different types of jumpers, choosing a "jump team," and how to recover once you've jumped and fallen.

In my life, I've had a few opportunities to jump my shadow – to do things that were a little risky, a little life changing and a lot uncomfortable. At the age of twenty-two I began my professional life as a classroom teacher. I had just gotten married and I took my new wife from Washington, DC to Atlanta, Georgia where I fell in love with the idea of teaching, training and shaping others. Of course I had no idea that my first group of students would be 5th graders – ten and eleven year olds who were, to be kind, *challenging*. To be perfectly honest, I believe that they had been spawned by their father Satan and sent to earth to torment me.

My mom had told me that life wasn't always going to be easy and I guess she was right. The beginning of this part of my story was already driving me crazy. These ten and eleven year olds would throw their bodies on the floor, run around like the possessed children of Lucifer and would never, ever, ever stop talking. Every day was a challenge. And every day I had to decide whether I was willing to jump my shadow to love and invest in these kids or take the easy way out and work on an oilrig somewhere. (A decidedly easier occupation, I had convinced myself.)

Somehow, I made it from 5th grade teacher to a middle-school supervisor, to a school administrator to a developer of educational programs for an organization of more than 50,000 students and teachers to now – where I own a research group and leadership institute and host international conferences throughout Europe and the Middle East. I've even had the chance to visit with government leaders, heads of organizations and terrorists (or freedom fighters, depending on one's point of view) to understand their stories and how their lives are shaping our world.

And I've learned a few things about jumping along the way, for example:

1. You can make jumps at any age, but it's easier when you're younger. You have less to lose, less at stake. But if you learn to jump when you're young, it's easier to jump throughout life. And your effectiveness grows as you gain experience and try new things.

2. Jumping can't be random – because if you jump just for the sake of jumping, you will not be jumping with purpose and are not likely to reach your goals.

3. Jumping your shadow is almost always scary. If someone tells you, "If it's the right thing to do, you'll just have peace about it," they are straight up crazy. I have never had internal peace about any of the significant jumps I've made. I usually knew what I was supposed to do, but it was never easy or "internally conflict free."

4. Sometimes when you jump, you land in a place that's unexpected. With people who are less than desirable to be around. It can make you want to stop jumping all together. But you won't and there's a lot that can be learned from these difficult situations.

5. Jumping brings great satisfaction if you do it for the right reasons - if you're living and jumping for something bigger than yourself.

But we'll talk about all of this as this book unfolds. I also want you to know that any parts of my story that I share aren't really so much about me, because I'm pretty ordinary. My story is more about what happens when you jump a series of shadows in pursuit of a meaningful life. In the end, the only person who can get credit for this is God. And finally, it's also important to remember that everyone has a life, but not everyone makes the jump. The choice is yours. It's your story to be told.

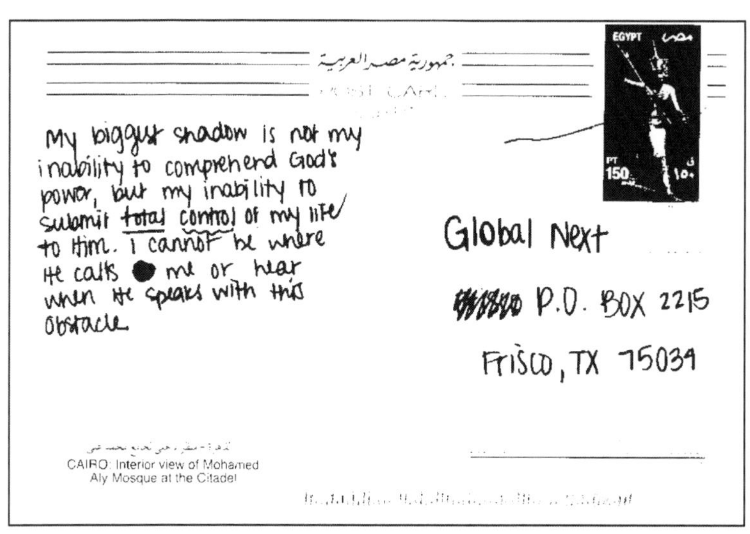

"My biggest shadow is not my inability to comprehend God's power, but my inability to submit <u>*total control*</u> *of my life to Him. I cannot be where He calls me or hear when He speaks with this obstacle."*

CHAPTER ONE
WHY BOTHER JUMPING?
SEEING OPPORTUNITIES IN A BROKEN WORLD

WHY BOTHER JUMPING?

Seeing opportunities in a broken world

I have a comfortable home and a beautiful wife. I have two sons who are interesting, funny and who enjoy spending time with me. I have a number of television shows that I find entertaining and I have a mildly unhealthy obsession with technological gadgets (especially if they come from the brilliant mind of Steve Jobs). I have no good reasons to leave my comfortable cocoon. It's warm, predictable and generally works for me. But except for the noble task of loving a wife and raising productive children, without any greater purpose, my comfortable life doesn't scrape against eternity. It's small. It's safe. And left as it is, my life wouldn't spill out onto much else.

And if I had kept the blinders on, if I had never wandered out of my comfort zone, I guess I could have stayed there. But a small, predictable life isn't the kind of life I want to live. I don't think it's the kind of life anyone should live. (And I'm not saying that you have to travel to the ends of the world or interview terrorists to live a big life – there are other things and other ways to do this in your own backyard.) I realize that when you choose to live a bigger life, you're asking for trouble. It does get complicated. It can be dangerous both physically and emotionally.

The Reason to Jump

I think that before you can decide you want to jump, you've got to know why it's important and valuable to jump. For me, when I look at the bigger picture, I see a world that is in need of hope. While I realize that I may not be able to change the whole world, I can impact individual lives. And those lives can go on to impact other lives. I feel the need to share the hope I have within me and to help others see hope and purpose for their lives – to resist the urge to see life as pointless and circumstances as random.

And when you take the time to pay attention, you'll see that our world is broken. That's one of the most compelling reasons to jump your shadow. Not as a thrill seeker, but as someone who recognizes the brokenness of our world and someone who wants to be part of the solution. Here's a quick (and incomplete) list of some of the issues that face our world today:

- Child Abuse
- Curing Disease
- Economic Issues
- Education
- Endangered Species
- The Environment
- Feeding The Hungry
- Fresh Water
- Genocide
- Healthcare
- Homelessness
- Human Rights

- Poverty
- Racism
- Terrorism
- Violence

The problem is that we often miss the broken world that is right in front of us. We are so absorbed in the minutia of our daily lives – the studying, the texting, the working, the Facebooking - that we miss the reason for jumping. We miss the importance of the human element. How can you make a difference if you don't identify the reason to jump? And how can we jump if we don't know what's important and what's not?

Missing What Matters

A couple of years ago I had taken a group of students to Oxford University in the UK for a leadership conference. On this particular day we were planning to visit Stonehenge and Shakespeare's hometown of Stratford. I went to meet the private coach driver who we'll call John - mostly because that was his name. And I was greeted by one of the surliest of Englishmen I had ever met. He was annoyed that he had to drive all the way from Oxford to Stonehenge and then to Stratford and then back to Oxford. I was slightly confused because this was sort of his purpose in life – to drive. He was a professional coach driver for goodness sake. And he was being paid to drive. So, I was baffled by his annoyance with doing his job. So, I invited him to simply do what he had been hired to do as I wasn't interested in a debate. He assured me that he generally kept to himself, so we wouldn't be engaging in any small talk. Duly noted.

Unfortunately, as soon as we had loaded the students on the bus and were heading towards the Salisbury plains, the coach driver decided that he had some stories to share. The first one began like this:

John: "So, back a few years ago, I had a girlfriend who was living with me. And one day she wanted to cook some fish in the frying pan."

Me: "Uh-huh."

John: "But I told her not to fry the fish because grease would splatter everywhere and I liked to keep a tidy kitchen."

Me: "Yeah, and then what?"

John: "She fried the fish and grease splattered everywhere just like I said it would."

Me: (Rousing myself from my coma) "Yeah, and then what?"

John: “Then I punched her in the mouth, broke up with her and kicked her out of the house.”

Me: (Fully out of my coma now) “WHAT??? Because she cooked the fish?”

John: “I told her not to.”

Me: “THEN WHAT???” (This had become a way better story than I had anticipated!)

John: “Oh, her brother and his friends came over and beat the snot out of me. But to be fair, I deserved it.”

Me: “Yeah, you deserved it! You hit the girl in the mouth! THEN WHAT?”

John: “Well, then I laid in wait for her brother with a baseball bat and started beating him in the head. I nearly killed him, but at the last moment, I thought, ‘You’re not worth it,’ so I called the police and turned myself in.” (Sidebar: I am always excited when someone used the phrase “laid in wait” in a normal conversation. It sounds so epic.)

Evidently John called the military police as he was in the British army. He was arrested, sentenced to seven days restriction and transferred to another base. That's it. End of story. All because of a fish.

Then John followed it up with another story. It went something like this:

John: "Now I'm married and we live in the country outside of London. Sometimes when we leave the windows open squirrels come into the house."

Me: "Yeah? Then what? (I was much more engaged in these stories now, because except for my general fear for the lives of my students on the bus, I was really enjoying myself now. And remember, every great story has some sort of conflict.)

John: "A couple of weeks ago my wife was working the night shift at the hospital. I was in bed with the lights off and I felt something on the bed. I took out my flashlight and saw there was a squirrel all settled down and sleeping on our comforter."

Me: "Yeah? THEN WHAT?" (I knew what he was capable of, so I was on the edge of my seat waiting to hear the inevitable story of him chasing this forest creature around his home with a machete.)

John: "Oh, nothing. It wasn't causing any harm, so I just let it spend the night."

Me: "WHAT???"

John: "Yeah, I mean I chased it out early in the morning, because you know, squirrels are notoriously incontinent, but otherwise, I just let it be."

OK, I have several things to say about this story. First of all, am I the only person who was unaware that squirrels were "notoriously" incontinent? Why had I never heard of this medical condition among the squirrel community? Why aren't the animal rights people looking for a cure for the small, weak bladders of squirrels? Apparently I am seriously out of the loop. I must not be following the right people on Twitter.

Secondly, why did this squirrel get such gentle treatment when the woman who John was supposedly in love with, got smashed in the face because she cooked fish and splattered grease in his kitchen. Obviously in John's economy of relationships, squirrels are more important than people. And when you recognize that squirrels are just rats with better clothes on, it becomes even more disturbing.

We live in a world where people pay attention to the wrong things and care about the wrong things. We don't recognize the needs of our world and the opportunities we have to be part of the solution. We think we're aware of everything around us, but this is not always the case. This was brilliantly demonstrated by a now-famous experiment conducted by Christopher Chabris and Daniel Simons.

Selective Attention

About twelve years ago, Chabris and Simons (2010) authors of the book, *The Invisible Gorilla: And Other Ways our Intuitions Deceive Us*, conducted an experiment that has gone on to be one of the best-know experiments in the psychological world. (You can see the video of the experiment yourself at www.theinvisiblegorilla.com) In the video experiment, the participants are asked to watch a short video where people in white shirts and black shirts are passing a number of basketballs. The task for the viewer is to count the number of passes made by those wearing white shirts to see if they can accurately count the passes.

Of course, counting the passes has little to do with the experiment. It's just a task to keep the viewers busy in order to gauge their attention. While the viewers are counting passes, a woman dressed in a gorilla suit walks through the players who are passing the basketballs. The gorilla stops, beats its chest and then continues to walk through the group.

At least 50% of those who view the video don't even see the gorilla. Which seems shocking because you'd think that a big gorilla walking through a group of people passing basketballs would certainly get your attention. But it doesn't. The researchers say that we don't see the gorilla because we don't expect a gorilla. Our brains are trained to see what we expect. (Which is also why people often miss seeing motorcycles on highways, because our brains are used to seeing cars, not motorcycles.) And evidently this selective attention problem has nothing to do with intelligence or gender. In every test, about 50% of the viewers missed the gorilla regardless of intellect (the original study was done at Harvard University) or whether they were male or female.

In another experiment conducted by Pulitzer Prize winner Gene Weingarten, (2007) world-famous violinist, Joshua Bell was asked to perform on his $3 million Stradivarius violin in a subway station in Washington, D.C. During the course of the experiment more than one thousand people passed by Bell, but only seven stopped to listen. Why weren't people paying attention? Why didn't people notice one of the world's foremost musicians giving a free concert? Probably because they were busy thinking about and attending to other things –like getting to work. No one expected Joshua Bell to be in a subway station playing amazing music. And because they weren't expecting it, they missed it.

But of those who stopped and listened, several did have one thing in common. In one-way or another they were experts in this area: they were either musicians themselves or they had been to one of Josh's concerts. In other words, their brains had already been prepped to notice Joshua Bell's musical genius. So, being an expert in a field can help you with your attention and your ability to be aware of things other might miss. Maybe zookeepers would notice a gorilla walking onto a basketball court more readily than the rest of us. So, perhaps our goal should be to become experts in recognizing shadows to be jumped and the opportunities the world affords us.

Becoming an Expert at World-Watching

When our attention is otherwise engaged we miss things that matter. We need to retrain our brain to notice what matters and then begin to take advantage of opportunities to jump our shadows and make a difference. We need to make unexpected events less unexpected. And the more you jump your shadow, the more likely you are to notice opportunities because they won't seem so unusual anymore – they become the normal way you look at life and live life.

Changing People's Situation

In their book, *Switch: How to Change Things When Change is Hard*, Dan and Chip Heath (2010) point out that if you want to change someone's behavior – in our case, if you want to change the way people recognize their shadows to jump and the destinations of global opportunity - you really need to change their situation. They say that what often looks like a problem with people is really a problem with our environment. If you want someone to start behaving in a different way, something needs to change about people's situation. And I believe that one way to do that is for those who have jumped their shadows to drag those who haven't jumped into situations that are new – situations that are compelling and life changing. (As we'll see in the next chapter that you also have to engage people's hearts and minds.) For some people, until they start seeing the broken world for themselves, until they start recognizing the obstacles in their life that must be jumped, they will simply wander through life missing what matters and missing opportunities to be part of something that can impact our world and individual lives. Which is a major reason why I drag people around the world through our leadership conference program, changing people's environment and "situation" so that they can experience change.

Recap:

1. We need to jump our shadows (get past our fears and weaknesses) because the world is broken and in need of hope.

2. Jumping your shadow will allow you to live a bigger, more meaningful life.

3. We miss opportunities to impact our world and live out our dreams because those types of opportunities are often unexpected. We miss the gorillas.

4. If you want to motivate yourself and others to jump and to recognize the opportunities available to all of us, we have to change people's situations.

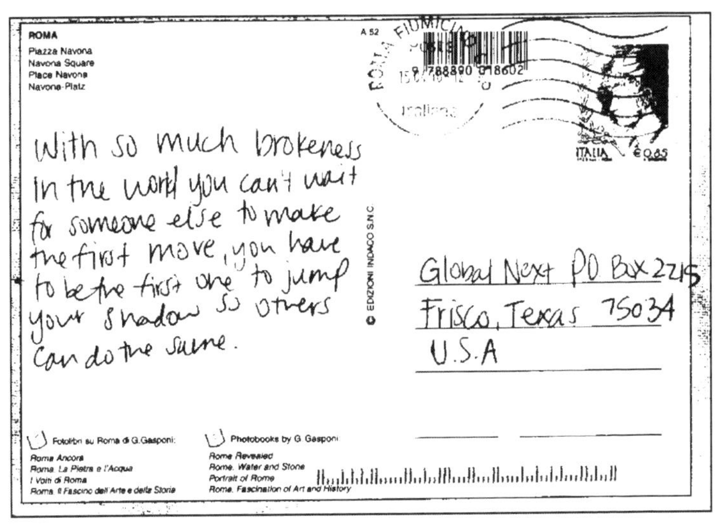

"With so much brokenness in the world you can't wait for someone else to make the first move, you have to be the first one to jump your shadow so others can do the same."

CHAPTER TWO
FEAR AND INTELLIGENCE
WHY SMART PEOPLE ARE AFRAID TO JUMP

FEAR AND INTELLIGENCE

Why smart people are afraid to jump

There are lots of things that scare us. According to MSN.com's *Health & Fitness* (Maloof, 2010), most of our fears are pretty universal. The most common fears include the fear of terrorism, flying, (this is probably more about crashing…) public speaking, heights, financial ruin, spiders, strange dogs, spaces (confined or open), and thunder and lightening storms. You'll notice that "death" didn't make the top nine. Perhaps that's because most of us feel that each of these top fears will "scare us to death," so there's no need to be redundant.

And then there are more specific (and unusual) fears, like the fear of gravity (barophobia) or the fear of beards (pogonophobia) or the fear of clowns (coulrophobia). Then there's neophobia. That's the fear of new things or new experiences. Maybe we all have a touch of this one. New things, change and different circumstances do seem to unsettle many people. And it's not so neurotic – it's usually based upon experience and a little personal research.

When I was considering moving away from Florida where I had a good job as the director of educational services for a large private school organization, I was nervous about taking a new position in another state. I was talking to my friend Robin, and she told me that it was normal to be afraid. She said, "Only smart people are afraid, because they understand the risk."

And that's probably very true. I don't know why I was thinking that making big, life-changing decisions would be easy or clear or drama free. Big decisions, choosing to change your life is not easy. And if you're even halfway intelligent, you know the potential cost of such choices.

But I also knew the consequences of doing nothing – which is a choice all by itself. If I wanted a big and meaningful life, I had to embrace the unknown. I had to start the jump even before I had complete certainty about how it would turn out. I was afraid. And there were plenty of reasons to be afraid.

Now, it's not that I was afraid that I would be jumping into a pit of spiders. And I'm certainly not afraid of public speaking. But I was nervous. I had a wife and kids that I wanted to be happy. And I had a good job and I was already doing things that mattered for others. The idea of walking away from something that was "pretty good" on the chance that I could experience the "extraordinary" was a risk I wasn't sure I wanted to take.

But here's what else I knew: I knew that over the previous eight years, I had finished everything I could do for the organization I was currently working with. There was no more that I could do that they wanted to do. I had also finally figured out (by attempting to be a "master of exclusion" and distinguishing between "good" things and "essential" things) what I was born to do. Yes, there were a number of things that I was good at – but being good at something doesn't mean that's what I was made for. So, after having identified my purpose, I was able to decide that in order to fulfill that purpose and to grow that purpose, I would have to jump. But that didn't make me feel any better. And if you're looking for everything to line up perfectly, you might not ever jump. Once in a while, things look obvious, secure and certain. More often than not, things look just flat out scary.

Knowing what I needed to do, I jumped. And it was a jump halfway across the country to Dallas, Texas where I learned many valuable and sometimes painful lessons. But I jumped. Even while I was still scared. And I found that God was still God, that He had a continuing purpose for my life and that He is faithful, even when people are not and the world seems unstable. In retrospect, had it not been for those first few years of partnering with another organization to continue developing my international leadership conferences, I would not be doing what I'm doing today. Here's what I learned about fear and intelligence:

5 Reasons Smart People Hesitate to Jump their Shadows:

1. **They know the cost.**
   No one said that jumping would be easy. Smart people can look down the road. They've catalogued what has happened to their friends and colleagues who were foolish enough to follow a dream or take a chance. They've read the horror stories of people who lost it all. And these stories have a way of sticking with smart people. Unfortunately, we don't always look at these stories and try to figure out where these other people went wrong. We look at them and say, "Well, that's a lesson for the kids out there – better to stay home and play it safe."

2. **They know the amount of work involved.**
   Smart people know that in order to accomplish anything worth accomplishing, it's going to take work. Lots of work. Hard work. And to be honest, most of us don't like the "prospect" of hard work. Especially if there's no guarantee of success at the end of it. If smart people are going to take risks, they prefer calculated risks.

3. **They know that some people will not understand.** Start jumping your shadow and you are guaranteed to have people around you asking questions and making comments. You know, simple little comments like, "Are you crazy?" "Why on earth would you do that?" "You're going to get your head cut off if you do that!" Of course they mean no harm. They just don't get it. And a lot of the time we get tired of explaining ourselves to people.

   When I speak at conferences across the US, I can always look out at the audience and pick out those people who get it and those who don't. After I talk about shadows I've jumped and where I've landed and the opportunities I've had, I sometimes get greeted by people who get excited (I like these people) and who want to either be a part of what I'm doing or have more insight into how they can jump their shadows for issues that matter to them.

   Then there are those who look at me and ask these kinds of questions, "If God had the good sense to have you born in America, why would you ever leave." (These people make me sad.) Or when they've heard about a great interview I've wrangled with some fascinating individual or organization they ask, "Why would they meet with *you*?" These people just frustrate me, because they don't get that it's not just about the interview (though sometimes those are pretty cool). It's about what else is going on in the context of these opportunities – in these cultures, in these places, the opportunities that God provides to touch people's lives.

4. **They know that it might take time to see the results of their efforts.**

   We live in an instant gratification world. We want it fast. We want it now. Smart people know that deep things take time. You might plant ideas and you might invest in people for years before you see results. And that's if you have the emotional strength not to give up. It can get discouraging.

   And I'll admit: I like quick results. It bugs me to see things move slowly. When I first went to Syria to try to interview an official from Hamas, I wanted results. I am somewhat passionate about getting honest viewpoints and first-person interviews regarding complicated issues. But I wasn't going to get those results during my first visit. In fact, I was denied my visa. (Some issue about the Syrian government not wanting somebody like me poking my nose in their business of what appeared to be state-sponsored terrorism.) I had to beg the Syrian ambassador to reconsider and let me into the country. I had to promise him that I wouldn't try to contact anyone from Hamas. Something about the Syrian government not being able to guarantee my safety. (Which, by the way, no one can guarantee anywhere at anytime. Security and safety exist only in the hands of God.)

So, when I arrived in Damascus, I immediately contacted the Ministry of Information. I wasn't planning to cause any trouble – it just seems like I had come an awfully long way not to get a little information and a little insight. By the time I had worked my way up to the head of the media department of the Ministry of Information, I was kicked out of the office after my first question. Fortunately for me I had previously stroked the ego of a guy in a lower position (that's a whole other art form for a completely different book) and he slipped me the phone number of a journalist that he thought might be able to help me. And he did – but it would take two years of developing that relationship to get a meeting with Talal Nasser, a head official of Hamas - a man who not only works in the PR aspect of Hamas, but also on the political side and is a co-founder of the military wing of Hamas. (You can read about this interview in the final chapter of this book.)

It took a while. Two years, another plane ticket, putting my life and safety into the hands of others. I got my meeting and I got my interview. But it wasn't like going through a drive-through window and ordering a happy meal.

5. **They know that they might fail.**
   Fear of failure is a huge issue for smart people. Well, actually for most of us. None of us likes to fail. But if you're going to jump your shadow and involve yourself in a bigger world, then you have to expect failure. Anyone who jumps is going to fall sometimes. But we'll talk more specifically about this in a later chapter.

Riders and Elephants

In the last chapter, I mentioned that Dan and Chip Heath (2010) suggest in their book *Switch*, that if you want people to change – and in our case – if we want to start jumping our shadows (or encouraging others to do the same) we have to change people's situation. What looks like a people problem, they say, is really a situational problem. Change someone's environment and you'll be able to change his life.

But they also state that if you really want to promote personal change, you have to impact people's hearts and minds. The Heath brothers draw on a classic metaphor that helps explain the struggle we all have in executing change in our lives. The metaphor actually comes from Jonathan Haidt's (2006) book, *The Happiness Hypothesis,* using the imagery of a Rider and an Elephant. The conflict of change comes down to the rub between your rational side (Rider) and your emotional side (Elephant).

Here's the problem: The Elephant likes instant gratification and short cuts. So when the Rider wants to do something new or difficult, (like exercise more, study harder, save money, improve your relationships or jump your shadow) the Elephant resists the idea. The Rider can pull the reins and force the Elephant to comply for a while, but the Elephant is just too big and strong. Eventually, the Rider just gets worn out! He may want to change, but his Elephant won't let him. One of the more interesting insights regarding change is that will power is an exhaustible resource (Heath and Heath 2010).

This principle was exemplified by an experiment conducted by a group of researchers that invited two groups of college students to participate in a "food perception" test. In reality, the researchers wanted to test the effect of forced self-control. In the lab were two different bowls. One bowl was filled with delicious, fresh-baked chocolate-chip cookies. The other bowl was filled with radishes. One group was asked to eat a couple of cookies – no radishes (not very difficult in the self-control area.) The other group was asked to eat a couple of radishes, but could not touch the cookies. (Much harder.)

The interesting part of the experiment came next. A new group of researchers came in to supposedly test the ability of college students over high school students to solve problems.

The two groups of college students were asked to complete some complex puzzles. What the researchers found was that the group who ate the cookies "spent nineteen minutes on the task, making thirty-four well-intentioned attempts to solve the problems. The radish-eaters were less persistent. They gave up after only eight minutes – less than half the time spent by the cookie eaters – and they managed only nineteen solutions attempts." (Heath and Heath 2010) Evidently, resisting the chocolate-chip cookies - exerting self-management is exhausting! And there's not much energy left for much else. Changing habits takes effort by the Rider – he needs to get the Elephant under control – and that's a lot of work. Tiring work.

But there are benefits to the nature of the Elephant. If your Elephant (emotions) is contemplating jumping your shadow, he's the one who will actually make the leap. If you want to jump your shadow, you've got to appeal to both the Rider and the Elephant. The Rider is your rational planner and strategist and your Elephant will be your cheerleader and jumper. Get them both going in the same direction and you're likely to jump your shadow, embrace risk, make profound changes and live a bigger, more purposeful life.

But if they are not working in harmony, the Rider gets exhausted as he tries to work against the natural, emotional reactions of the Elephant. It's not so much that the Rider is lazy or unable to follow through on what he says he wants to accomplish, he's just worn out! It's hard to control an Elephant! But if you can break through to the emotional side – and motivate your Elephant - the side that cares and becomes passionate – then you are no longer exhausted when it comes to making changes. But, if the Elephant isn't sure what direction to go in, he will just run around in circles. That's why the Rider needs to provide clarity and direction. (Heath and Heath 2010) The clearer the path, the more well-defined the destination and the immediate path, the more cooperative you will find your Elephant. If the Elephant and Rider work together change is possible. With practice, you can retrain both the Rider and the Elephant to wisely participate in jumping shadows and taking risk and participating in a bigger life.

Recap

1. Smart people know the costs and consequences of taking risks, so they are less likely to take them.

2. Our rational intellect (Rider) may be telling us to move forward, but our emotions (Elephants) are more powerful and tend to control us, making us overly excited or overly fearful - less than productive.

3. If you can get your Rider and Elephant working together, then change is possible and shadows will be jumped.

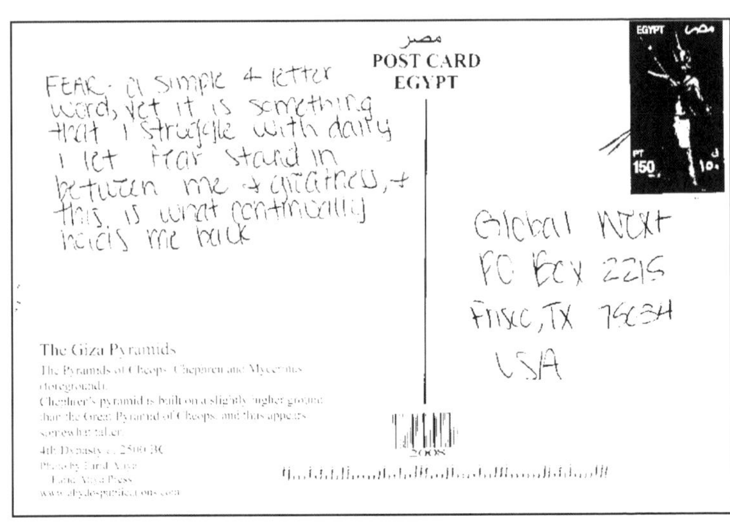

"Fear: a simple 4-letter word, yet it is something that I struggle with daily. I let fear stand in between me and greatness and this is what continually holds me back."

CHAPTER THREE
QUESTIONS AND JUMPERS
KNOW THE PLAYERS

QUESTIONS AND JUMPERS

Know the Players

When it comes to the idea and practice of jumping our shadows, we're all different. We all respond to the challenges and hesitations differently and we've all been impacted by our histories – our previous stories that have shaped the way we look at risk and opportunity. Before we can become successful, productive jumpers, we need to ask a few questions. These questions, if answered honestly, will tell you (and others) a lot about the way you think and view the world.

Three Pre-Jump Questions

1. **What do I have to jump?**
   What's your issue? What is holding you back from living a big life? For some, it's fear, uncertainty, procrastination, apathy or lack of vision. For others it might be selfishness, an emotional issue, awful habits, or maybe you're just having a series of bad hair days and that's what's holding you up. But you have to identify what is it that's keeping you from jumping – and reaching your life's potential.

It's better if you're just honest with yourself – and recognize the fears or habits that are working against you. In fact, I'd rather have someone just tell me, "I don't really care," or "I'm comfortable as I am." I don't like hearing that, but at least it's honest. And if this is the case, all I can say is, "Good luck with that – now, please move out of the way – because there's stuff that's got to be done!" You can't force people to jump. You *can* guilt people into action and you *can* momentarily inspire people to jump. But you cannot babysit people and keep them caring and keep them motivated. No, that comes from somewhere deep inside of them. And we will talk about that in another chapter – the issue of what really motivates us.

I know that some people would like me to park here and give you solutions to overcoming your horrible habits, your fear of flying or your pattern of procrastination. But here's my deal: I'm not a therapist. And I have a really simple way of looking at these things. Once you know the truth (that there is a world in need of hope and that a small life is not satisfying) then you need no further instructions to proceed. Just do it. Decide to be somebody. We all have weaknesses. We've all been damaged. We all have issues and excuses. I don't want to sound insensitive, but one of the biggest wastes of your time is defining yourself by life's hurts or your weaknesses or your baggage. You are much more than your worst moments. You are infinitely more valuable than what has hurt you.

When you stop identifying yourself by life's difficulties, then you are in a position to start living and serving and helping. Start talking to people who have jumped and who have done things that matter. Follow these people around. Figure out what they did and how they did it. Get over yourself and reach out for God's grace – grace that is available for those who want it. And then get on with it.

2. **For whom am I jumping?**

Are you jumping for yourself or for something bigger than yourself? Most of us are motivated by what we think is good for us. In fact, most people spend most of their lives doing things for themselves. But I have to wonder, in the story of your life, is there no one else in it except for you? Is there no broader story line where your choices and your life spill out onto those around you, leaving people different and changed?

I'm not against fun. I'm not against exciting experiences. But I am fully aware that we live in a global culture that easily gets stuck in the hedonistic moment at the expense of purpose and meaning. Sometimes in the pursuit of our goals, our success accidently spills out into the world.

But accidental spillage, while the world will take it, is not the same as someone who manages their pursuits for the purpose of something greater than personal gain.

Do you want to know whom you're jumping for? Ask yourself these questions and it will become pretty obvious:

1. I want to achieve an impressive professional position so that I can:
   A. Feel awesome about myself and my accomplishments.
   B. Use it as a platform to influence others for change.

2. I want to have a million dollars in the bank by the time I'm thirty so that I:
   A. Can feel safe and secure.
   B. Can use it for projects and people to improve their opportunities and life.

3. I want to achieve personal popularity in order to:
   A. Feel loved and valuable.
   B. Use my influence to persuade others to reach their potential.

You're smart. You already know that if you chose the first options you are probably jumping and taking risks to achieve things that satisfy you and that revolve around you. If you gravitated towards the second option, you tend to see the bigger picture. You recognize that when you jump, when you achieved your goals, those achievements and that success are tools- something to be used as leverage to impact others and to change the world.

3. **To where am I jumping?**

   It's not enough to just jump. You have to have a destination in mind. That does not mean that you have every single detail figured out. In my experience, things change along the way to the final destination. In fact, when I look back on my jumps, I don't know that I could have predicted the end at the beginning. When people (people who might just look at certain aspects of my life) ask me what it's like to have achieved my dreams, my answer would have to be that I would never have dreamed this big – ever. In my dreams, I would not have imagined the places I've seen, the people I've met or the rare opportunities I've had. But I always knew the general direction I was headed. I just didn't always know how I was going to get there, what the places would look like or foresee the interesting stops along the way. Sometimes all we can see is one jump at a time.

Types of Jumpers

Once you have struggled through these three questions, it's time to look at jump styles. Most of us will approach jumping our shadows in our own unique ways – some styles more effective than others. Hopefully, with practice, our jumps will improve. Sometimes all it takes to have greater jumping success is a small shift in your thinking. Just one "aha" moment where everything suddenly becomes clear. Perhaps you'll see yourself in the examples below.

1. **Bench warmer:** You sit out most jumps. You love to watch other people jump. You "think" about jumping all the time – but you rarely do it. You love the "idea" of jumping but for you, it seems like your comfort zone is acceptable – why cause trouble? Why take a risk? You sometimes live vicariously through the jumps of others.

   Life changing thought: In the end you will have more regrets about sitting than you will have regrets about occasional hurts and failure.

2. **Short Jumper:** You choose to jump. You start well. You run fast. You jump hard. But you rarely get considerable distance and you fall to earth far too early. This can frustrate you and frighten you into not taking future risks. Sometimes this is due to considerable baggage that you're carrying. You might have confused "jumping your shadow" with "packing up all your shadow issues

and taking them with you." It's hard to jump far when you're not jumping "over" your weaknesses but rather trying to jump "with" your weaknesses.

Life changing thought: Let go of the past. It's easier to jump if you release some of your baggage.

3. **Hesitant jumper:** You're right up to the jump line. You understand the line that must be crossed. You see a glimpse of the goal at the other end. And you wait. And wait. And watch. And look. And wait. Then you sit. Maybe tomorrow. There's always tomorrow.

   Life changing thought: Waiting is for people who are dead.

4. **Random jumper:** You jump all the time. You jump for everything. You jump for any and all opportunities. You make people nervous. You talk about jumping here and there and you're always starting this and that. You jump in. You jump out. You are exhausting.

   Life changing thought: Activity doesn't necessarily mean that you're changing the world. Being busy doesn't mean you're being productive.

5. **High Jumpers:** You aim high. You want it all. You dream big. You reach for the impossible and eventually you go for it. But sometimes your dreams are so lofty

and your expectations are so high that there is no way you can actually achieve your goals. At least not as you've dreamed and envisioned them.

Life changing thought: Dreams are inspiring – as long as you can survive them.

6. **Pole Vaulter:** You aim higher. You use others to accomplish your jumps. This is not the same as partnering with others. Using people means you have little regard for them and their work. Partnering means that you can accomplish more together than either of you can alone. A big difference in mentality. Using people as poles is not cool.

   Life changing thought: People matter. Your accomplishments can be measured by how they impact those around you.

7. **Distance jumper:** You jump long. You jump the distance. You reach and surpass your goals. You make it – you change it – you do it. You change your life and you change the world.

   Life changing thought: To become a distance jumper is a lifestyle – not a one-time event.

In the end, the primary difference between types of jumpers, I believe, is how they view their choices in life.

Fundamentally, it comes down to how you look at the freedom you have to choose a purposeful path in this life. Do you believe that you have the freedom to make choices about your life and the freedom to think differently about those choices? Or do you think that life is fated for you and that you have no active role in shaping your story? In our next chapter, we'll talk about the art of choice and how your concept of freedom fundamentally changes your direction in life.

Recap:

1. It's important to know the what, why and where before you start your jump.

2. If you're going to jump, it should be worthy of your effort and worthy of the world's needs.

3. Jumping for distance is better than falling short or waiting around.

4. If you can shift your thinking, you can shift your jump quality. As is true for many sports, it's mostly a mental game.

TOSCANA

One time I wasn't
strong in my faith
and I missed my moment
and I think about it all
the time

Global Next
PO Box 2215
Frisco Texas 35034

499

"One time I wasn't strong in my faith and I missed my moment and I think about it all the time."

CHAPTER FOUR
JUMPING YOUR SHADOW
CHOOSING TO LIVE A BIG LIFE

JUMPING YOUR SHADOW

Choosing to live a big life

Some people measure their lives in minutes, days and years. I prefer to mark life by the choices I've made - choices that have shaped me and shaped my future. But it's hard to make interesting choices when you're paralyzed with fear. It's also hard to make interesting choices when you aren't aware that you *can* make choices. The central purpose of this book is to convince you to jump your shadow. To help you open your eyes and see the needs of the world, to see the limitless potential of your life and to do something about both! I've explained how broken this world is that we're living in. We've discussed the fact that changing your mindset to jump is not easy, especially when your Rider (intellect) and Elephant (emotions) aren't in sync. Now it's time to get into the very heart of the book – the art of choosing to jump and choosing a big life. How does one choose to jump his shadow? There are three factors: First, you have to understand that you have choices. Second, you must balance your individualist and collectivist worldviews. And finally, you must rid yourself of your inner victim.

Rats, Dogs and Individualism

Curt Richter, a psychobiology researcher from John Hopkins School of Medicine conducted an interesting experiment back in 1957. Now, I'll warn you, those of you who have a soft spot for rats, will not like this experiment. It never ends well for the rats. For those of you who think that the world will be just fine with fewer rats, read on:

The study, as told by Sheena Iyengar (2010) in her book, *The Art of Choosing,* was designed to study the effects of water temperature on endurance. Richter and his associates put rats in jars of water to see how long they would swim before giving up and drowning. The rats were also subjected to jets of water from above to prevent them from just floating and taking the easy way out of survival. Using rats of similar physical ability, Richter was surprised to find that some rats swam for 60 hours before drowning while others gave up and drowned after 15 minutes. Why were some of the rats so determined to survive while others appeared to have no interest in the struggle for life?

For the next stage of the experiment, the researchers did something different before subjecting the rats to the sink or swim test. First, they repeatedly held the rats firmly in their hands but allowed them to eventually wriggle free. Then they placed the rats in the jars of water, let them swim for their lives and then released them and put them back in their cages. After doing this repeatedly, the rats were put back in the jars of water for the final test to see how they would respond to the final challenge. This time, every rat swam for a minimum of 60 hours. Not one rat gave up early. Now, it's true – they all died. But that's science for you. But the interesting question is this – is it possible that these rats who experience their version of "hope" came to believe that when faced with difficulty that they had a choice about survival and success? Is it possible that some people, like some rats are natural survivors because something inside of them understands the power of hope and the power of choice – the choice to live, the choice to survive, the choice to jump over their fears and pursue something greater?

Sheena Iyengar shares another experiment that is significant. The experiment, involving a group of mongrel dogs, was performed in 1965 by Martin Seligman of Cornell University and changed the way people view choice and control. The first part of the experiment subjected pairs of dogs to electrical shocks (painful, but apparently non-damaging). Both dogs in the pair were subjected to the same shock for the same amount of time. The difference was that one dog of the pair could end the shock by pressing the side panels with its head and the other could not turn off the shock no matter what it did. Over repeated shocks, the dogs that could stop the shocks showed annoyance, but learned pretty quickly how to expect and end the pain by pressing the side panels. The dogs that couldn't control the shocks showed great signs of anxiety and depression.

As Ms. Iyengar tells it, "In the second phase of the experiment, both dogs in the pair were exposed to a new situation to see how they would apply what they'd learned from being in – or out of - control. Researchers put each dog in a large black box with two compartments, divided by a low wall that came up to about shoulder height on the animals. On the dog's side, the floor was periodically electrified. On the other side, it was not. The wall was low enough to jump over, and the dogs that had previously been able to stop the shocks quickly figured out how to escape. But of the dogs that had not been able to end the shocks, two-thirds lay passively on the floor and suffered." (Iyengar, 2010)

These "victimized" dogs didn't realize they had a choice. Even when they saw the other dogs jumping the wall and even when the researchers dragged the dogs over to the other side and "showed" them where freedom was, they still gave up and accepted the pain. This is interesting in that it appears that when you are taught through experience that you have no control, even when you are given freedom, you may not take it. It then stands to reason that some people, for whatever reason, are convinced at some point that they can make the important jumps in life and even though they know there will be pain and discomfort, they "choose" their way through it and beyond it. Others, meanwhile, even if they see others jump, even if you show them where they could jump, don't apply or recognize that freedom for themselves.

The mental aspect of making choices is powerful. The importance of shifting your thinking so that you can choose to jump is vital. When you think you have no control over your life and choices, or more likely, because your experiences have convinced you that you have limited control, it produces stress, and not productivity – like the stress exhibited by caged animals in zoos – even when they are provided with beautiful surroundings.

Individualism v. Collectivism

The subject of how you view freedom of choice is further impacted by cultural factors. Dutch organizational sociologist, Geert Hofstede studied the interactions between national cultures and organizational cultures. Professor Hofstede conducted perhaps the most comprehensive study of how values in the workplace are influenced by culture. Hofstede analyzed a large database of employee values scores collected by IBM between 1967 and 1973 covering more than 70 countries and 3 regions. Hofstede's study demonstrates that there are consistent characteristics of national and regional cultural groupings that affect the behavior of societies as well as organizations. For our discussion of how your view of choice impacts how willing you are to jump your shadow, the rankings of national groups' view of individualism and collectivism is particularly interesting.

If you grew up in a culture that scores high on the "collectivism" scale, like Asia or the Middle East, you are more likely to be a person who considers the needs of the group more than your own individual achievement. But you are also more likely to view your choices as limited and to downplay your ability to self-determine and make a difference as an individual.

However, if you grew up in an "individualistic" nation, like the US, Australia or Western Europe, you are more likely to view your life as one with multiple choices and lots of freedom, but you may also miss the importance of jumping your shadow for the benefit of others.

The global average score for individualism is 64 out of 100. (The higher the score, the more "individualistic" your worldview is. The lower the score, the more you lean toward "collectivism" and the importance of the group) The US scores a 91 followed by Australia at 90 and the United Kingdom at 89. These are nations that place great importance on individual achievement and personal responsibility. Latin American countries rank lower on this scale, with Argentina being a typical example scoring a 50 on the individualism scale. In most Latin American nations, the group is as important or slightly more important than individual achievement. Arab nations, like Egypt scored a 38 indicating a preference for collectivism. And China and South Korea score even lower with a 24 and 18 respectively, indicating an even stronger preference for the group. (Hofstede, 2003. See all national ranks at: http://www.geert-hofstede.com/index.shtml)

Finding the Balance

It is easy to feel strongly drawn towards the cultural worldview in which you grew up. It's the same feeling we have towards favorite songs that were popular on the radio when we fell in love, TV shows we loved when we were children or the taste of your mom's cooking. It's part of the fabric of who you are – it's hardwired into your brain. But for those who want to jump all shadows that hinder your optimal effectiveness, we must seek balance. Either of these views, taken to an extreme, can potentially limit your global outlook. While individualism can inspire great personal achievement, if left unchecked, you will pursue only those things that benefit you personally and you will miss the opportunities to invest in people and issues outside of yourself. Collectivism feels a great responsibility to the group – you instinctively recognize the needs of those around you and will sacrifice for their sake. At the same time, without recognizing your personal responsibility to take risk and to jump your individual shadows, you can end up feeling powerless to make choices and to make an individual difference.

Growing up in Washington, D.C., visiting the Washington National Zoo was a favorite elementary school field trip. One year, for some reason, buying peacock feathers was the "in" thing to do. So we all bought them. And then we spent our time after school seeing how long we could balance them on our fingers. Contests erupted. Lunch money was wagered. Trash talk filled the air as my friends vied for the coveted position of "peacock feather master." (We were a pathetic group, I admit.)

But in the end, I learned something about balance. If, in the attempt to balance my peacock feather on my finger, I did absolutely nothing, then my feather would fall definitively to one extreme or the other. It would fall hard to the right or hard to the left. In order to keep the feather upright and balanced, I had to put forth effort. I had to make constant adjustments. I had to be aware of every element that was pulling on my feather. Finding and maintaining balance in life requires work, being observant and making constant adjustments. And when we achieve a balance in our thinking regarding collectivism and individualism, then we can exhibit the best of both worldviews. We can feel the freedom to make choices, recognize that each of us has a personal responsibility to live a life of purpose and we can also recognize the importance of living and striving for things bigger than our personal desires and satisfaction. We can recognize the importance of living a life that impacts others – and that strives to meet the needs of a broken world.

Faith and Freedom

Cultural worldviews are fascinating in how they impact our thinking. So what about views on religion? Does having a strong religious foundation or belief system that includes standards, rules and limits constrain your choices and thereby make you less likely to take personal responsibility for your life and jumps? Does it create fatalism? Does following a strict religious code box you in too much? The answer is surprising.

For nearly two years, Sheena Iyengar interviewed over 600 people from nine different religions. As she describes it, "These faiths were categorized as fundamentalists (Calvinism, Islam, and Orthodox Judaism), which imposed many day-to-day regulations on their followers; conservatives (Catholicism, Lutheranism, Methodism, and Conservative Judaism); or liberal (Unitarianism and reformed Judaism), which imposed the fewest restrictions." (Iyengar, 2010) Throughout her research, the participants of these faiths filled out three different surveys and reflected on the impact of religion on their lives, their choices and even their optimism. Surprisingly (at least to the researcher) it turned out that those of more fundamentalist beliefs (the faiths with the greatest restrictions on behavior) exhibited greater optimism and hope and less fatalism when faced with life's difficulties. Evidently the group most susceptible to depression and feeling pessimistic was the most liberal group – those with the fewest restrictions. (Iyengar, 2010)

While, this came as a surprise to the researcher, it does not surprise me. As a Christian who believes that God is sovereign and that following His will brings greater stability and happiness, it makes perfect sense. The combination of knowing you have choices, that you are not a victim combined with an understanding that you are connected to something greater than yourself is a powerful combination. Rather than creating restrictions, having a code of standards can provide the framework in which to live and think. It actually can provide greater freedom because your world has boundaries, order and purpose – which surprisingly provide more liberty rather than less. In other words, I have the freedom to subject myself to my belief system and voluntarily choose higher standards. This does not limit me – in fact, in my worldview – and the worldview of many others, this frees me. It frees me to live a bigger life. Believing that God is ultimately in control means that by following His standards I will find ultimate purpose and meaning. Rather than looking at my faith as limiting and restrictive, I look at the choice of follow God as liberating.

Recognizing that you have choice is good. Strong religious beliefs don't inhibit you from jumping or experiencing freedom. So what is it that causes many people to sit out life's jumps and miss opportunities? I believe it has a lot to do with your internal dialogue – whether or not you are constantly telling yourself that you are a victim. Do you believe that you are a casualty of circumstances or do you believe that you can control – choose – the type of life, purpose and impact you want to have.

Getting Rid of Your Inner Victim

I was sitting in a coffee shop in Cairo with about 15 university students. We were having a great conversation about life and purpose and doing things that mattered. I brought up the issue of victimhood and gave my little speech about how damaging it is for people to internally view themselves as victims of their circumstances. When I finished my argument, one of the young men looked at me and said, "Dr. Phil, I'm sorry, but I don't think you understand. Life is harder for us here in Egypt. We don't have the kinds of choices and opportunities that you have had. In many ways, we are victims."

And in that one statement lays the problem. It's the idea that your circumstances dictate how you think and how you think determines how big your life is. It also reveals the idea that jumping your shadow and living a meaningful life can only be done with limitless money and professional opportunities. So, I told him a story. A story I heard a long time ago that changed the way I thought about life, obstacles and difficulties. The story comes from the life of a woman named Corrie ten Boom. She was a Dutch woman in her early fifties when an opportunity came to her. At the height of World War 2 and the Nazi occupation of Holland, Corrie and her sister and father were asked to help protect people. To hide people who the Nazis wanted to kill – simply because of who these people were and what they believed. It was a big shadow to jump. It was a shadow that most people in their 50's would never even consider. But Corrie didn't look at her life in terms of years and limitations. She looked at what needed to be done and recognizing the needs of others, she jumped. And because of her jump, lives were saved.

But eventually, the secret that the ten Boom family was hiding people from the Nazis was betrayed. The Gestapo came and arrested Corrie, her sister Betsie and her father and took them to prison. Fortunately, the group of people who were hiding in the house at the time were not discovered and escaped to freedom. But physical freedom was not to be for Corrie and her family. Her father died shortly after being arrested. And the sisters ended up in Ravensbruck, a notorious women's concentration camp in northern Germany.

Taken from their home and stripped of their dignity and freedom, these middle-aged women could have been bitter and disappointed with how their lives turned out. They jumped their shadow to help people they didn't even know and this is what they got for their sacrifice? How could it possibly be worth it? And yet, because they refused to think of themselves as victims, they remained free, even while in prison. At every turn they saw opportunities to bring hope and help to other prisoners. And because of their belief in God and His ultimate control, they knew they were free to respond with love and grace even under the most unthinkable conditions.

While in prison, Betsie, never physically strong to begin with, became very ill. But as her body grew weaker, her hope – her internal freedom - never wavered. While lying on a stretcher outside in the freezing temperatures of Ravensbruck, waiting for what passed as medical attention, Bestie had Corrie lean down to hear these whispered words, "...must tell people what we have learned here. We must tell them that there is no pit so deep that He is not deeper still. They will listen to us, Corrie, because we have been here."

Corrie stared at the wasted form of her sister and asked, "But when will all this happen, Betsie!"

"Now. Right away. Oh, very soon! By the first of the year, Corrie we will be out of prison!" (Ten Boom, 1984)

And they were. Betsie's freedom came with a coffin. But she ended her life as she had lived it – participating in something greater than herself. Corrie was miraculously released from prison and spent the rest of her life traveling around the world talking to groups of people about the importance of forgiveness.

After telling this story to the group of students in the coffee house in Cairo, I looked at the young man who said that I didn't understand and that he was indeed a victim of his circumstances and I said to him, "If these middle-aged women did not think that they were victims in a Nazi concentration camp, if Corrie ten Boom could live out the rest of her life encouraging people to forgive those who had hurt her and her family, then you, sir, are in no position to think of yourself as a victim."

And he agreed. He had to. Nazi concentration camp stories are perspective re-setters. And sometimes we need that to realize that we have more freedom than we realize. And that we are only victims to the extent that we allow ourselves to be. When you refuse to be a victim, you choose freedom. And when you know you have freedom, you are free to jump just about anything.

Recap:

1. Recognize the power of choice. When you know you have the freedom to make choices, use that freedom to shape your life.

2. Find balance for your worldview of individualism and collectivism. Balance will allow you to dream of what you can accomplish and accomplish things that will impact others.

3. Stop being a victim. Life doesn't happen "to" you unless you let it.

ROMA - Città del Vaticano
Cappella Sistina
Michelangelo. La Creazione dell'Uomo
particolare

ROMA FIUMICINO CMP
Poste Italiane
15.04.10 - 12

ITALIA €0,85

I know God has
designed me to
be a masterpiece.
I need to keep
chipping away the
sin in my life to
reveal the masterpiece
He has created me to be.

"I know God has designed me to be a masterpiece. I need to keep chipping away the sin in my life to reveal the masterpiece He has created me to be."

CHAPTER FIVE
MOTIVATIONAL FORCES
WHAT MAKES YOU JUMP?

MOTIVATIONAL FORCES

What makes you jump?

Harry Harlow was a scientist who conducted experiments back in the 1940's that began to poke holes in the accepted wisdom of what motivates people. Harlow, of the University of Wisconsin, performed experiments with rhesus monkeys to measure their ability to learn. In his experiment, the monkeys had to solve a three-step mechanical puzzle. By the 14th day of the experiment, these monkeys had figured out the puzzle and were performing it more and more quickly. The interesting thing was that they were doing it, apparently for the fun of it. They had never received any rewards for their efforts. They were given no food, affection or praise. It appeared as if they were solving the puzzle for the sheer satisfaction of completing the challenge. (Pink 2009)

The "Third Drive"

Most people have long believed that when it comes to motivation, people are driven by two forces: biological urges or outside "extrinsic" motivators. The options seemed to be that people would either be motivated by food, water or sex or they would be motivated by reward or punishment. Back in the 1930's, B. F. Skinner, the Harvard clinical psychologist, made a career out of demonstrating that you could condition behavior based on a system of rewards and punishments.

But Harry Harlow was seeing something different. He noted that these monkeys were motivated by something else. They were not being driven by their need for food, water or sex. They were not being given rewards for completing the puzzles or punished for not completing the puzzles. They were doing it for the love of the puzzles. This is what started the idea of the "third drive," what we now call "intrinsic motivation." In fact, when Harlow introduced "extrinsic rewards" to the monkeys in the form of food as an incentive, it served to disrupt the performance – more mistakes were made and the monkeys solved fewer puzzles.

A few decades later, another scientist, Edward Deci of Carnegie Mellon University, picked up where Harlow left off. He performed a series of experiments where people had to solve a series of puzzles. Some groups solved the puzzles for free. Other groups solved some of the puzzles for free and other puzzles for payment. What he found was that when people were solving the puzzles for free, their intrinsic motivation stayed pretty constant – they remained interested in the work and in the challenge of the work. The competition of the puzzle seemed to be enough to motivate them to solve it. But for the group of participants that were paid for some puzzles and not paid for others, Deci found something surprising. Paying people to solve the puzzles resulted in intensified interest and better performance – for the short-term. Because when those same participants were told that they would not be paid for the next day's puzzles, their interest in the puzzles diminished to levels lower than the first day of the experiment when they were also not paid. What Deci learned (and confirmed in a couple of additional experiments) was that when people were motivated by money for some activities, the "intrinsic motivation" for the activity became lost – which indicated that in some cases, rewards had a negative effect. (Pink 2009)

Motivation is a funny thing. It seems to spring to life for some things and not for others. It can be fueled and can jump ahead and it can wither and go dormant. Numerous studies have shown that while external motivators work for some things – rewards do not work for everything and often they can have the opposite effect and actually lower motivation.

Now to be sure – you can't go through life expecting people to do everything for free. You can't assume that people will just rise to the challenge like they're editing a Wikipedia entry – just for the love of it. Studies have shown that if people's basic needs aren't met (like enough money to pay their bills and enough positional satisfaction at work) they will be so distracted by the idea of survival that motivation and focus become disrupted and not much is accomplished.

Rewards can and do work. Just not all the time. And probably less often than you think they do. While rewards might work well for really boring tasks, my hunch is that for the majority of important shadows that you will jump and the purposes for jumping those shadows, no amount of money will do the trick – at least not in the long term. There has to be another motivator. Something deeper. Something more enduring.

Peter Block, a management thinker and writer makes a brilliant point. He believes that conditioning people based on extrinsic motivators has created a culture of entitlement where workers are willing to negotiate their commitment for a dollar value. Jane Strickler (2006) quotes Block as saying, "I am willing to do what is rewarded. I want desperately to know what they (the management) value. I refuse to do what is not rewarded, and I want greater rewards, especially when I deliver greater and greater results. Ultimately, no level of reward is enough, for my work, and my purpose has become a game. Winning more becomes the point, for I need the game to feel valued. What I may not realize is that when I choose this path, I sacrifice my own purpose. Everything is offered up for auction, the most precious of which is our own freedom."

The significant finding of the studies of researchers Harlow and Deci is that intrinsic motivation – the motivation that is fueled from inside you – is rather fragile. It's powerful, engaging and moving, but it is also hard to coax out and it easily goes into hiding. It really needs the right environment to flourish.

Back in the days when I was teaching school, I decided that I would distract my students with a classroom pet. I bought a gerbil. They loved it. And I loved the fact that they had something to focus on besides bringing on my early nervous breakdown.

One morning when I came into the classroom, I was assaulted by an unpleasant odor that reminded me that the gerbil's cage hadn't been cleaned in a while. I figured I might as well take care of that before the students arrived. I reached into his glass cage and picked him up so that I could clean out his home. And what did I get for my helpful gesture? The son-of-a-mouse bit me! Hard! And so I dropped him. Not knowing what else he had up his furry little sleeve, I decided to use an empty box to trap him, scoop him up and deposit him back in his cage – a home that I had now determined was far too good for him.

So in a YouTube-worthy performance, I chased the gerbil around the room with this box. I finally cornered him near a wall and quickly and decisively brought the box down over him. Only I didn't quite get all of him in the box. Only the back half of him. And I admit, I must have been filled with adrenalin, because I brought that box down pretty hard. And as I looked at him, his head and upper arms were outside the box, while the rest of him was inside the box. And he looked surprised. And I was surprised. And I lifted up the box and he ran around in three circles, fell over and died.

Now there were two lessons that were learned that day. Lesson number one was important for my students: You don't mess with a teacher who's already killed once that day. (I had amazing schoolyard street-cred after murdering a beloved classroom pet. No one was going to mess with me after this incident!) Lesson number two was this: Some things in life are fragile. And that lesson can be applied to many things in life – from your dreams and hopes to your integrity and relationships – to the power of your intrinsic motivation.

When you understand how fragile intrinsic motivation is to begin with, you begin to understand the enormity of Peter Block's statement. We're selling our purpose for cash. We're trading in our internal fire of what matters for something that can't possibly last or stand the test of time. No wonder men who play professional sports suddenly forget their love of the game and trade that in for the love of a new game: The game of increased financial gain. How many times have we seen players refuse to play the sport they say they love in order to hold out for a few more dollars? Their intrinsic love for the game – the love that motivated them through all those practices – has now been replaced with another game – the game of negotiating for more money. And in the process, and on so many different levels outside of the business world and the sports world, we can no longer find the internal fire to pursue things that we should love – things that should matter. In the end, we have traded in our freedom for a temporary payoff. And as we have already noted, recognizing one's freedom of choice is an important factor in the success of being able to make life jumps.

Getting the Feeling Again

So, how can we get the feeling again? How can we rekindle our intrinsic motivation and have the courage and conviction to jump? And to keep jumping? And to jump for what matters? According to Daniel Pink (2009) in his book *Drive: The Surprising Truth About What Motivates Us*, there are three elements that generate and help to sustain intrinsic motivation: Autonomy, mastery and purpose. Let's take a look at each factor:

1. **Autonomy**.

   Autonomy is the idea that we work better if we're self-directed – that people perform better when they have some freedom about what they do, when they do it, who they do it with and how they do it.

On a flight from Atlanta to Dallas I was talking to a young man sitting next to me on the plane. He was working for a software company that designs video games. As we talked, it was obvious that he was passionate about what he did. And why not – he loved computers and he loved games. As he described his working environment to me, I was surprised and sort of fascinated. It seemed as if there were almost no traditional workplace standards. People dressed as they pleased and were free to come and go as they pleased. They could eat there, they could sleep there and they could leave when they wanted. So, I said to him, “Wow, that sounds amazing, but really loose. How does the CEO ensure that things get done with so much freedom available?”

He looked at me and said, “We’re all so thankful and lucky to have this job, that we’d never dream of messing it up. Everyone that I work with is motivated from the inside. In fact, we are so internally motivated, that we don’t need anything motivating us from the outside. We don’t look at it as if we’re free to get away with stuff. We look at it as if we are free to design and build the best video games ever." And that leads me to the second element that can sustain intrinsic motivation: Mastery.

2. **Mastery**.
The pursuit of mastering something provides internal momentum that always leans forward and pulls you towards your shadows, over your shadows and to your jump destination. And this begins when you are doing what you were made to do - just like the guy who was designing video games. He loved it, he was good at it, and he was passionate about it. And he was pursing the mastery of it. Understanding yourself and your gifts and then plugging those abilities into the right areas of your vocation, relationships and service, allows you to pursue getting better at what you're already good at and interested in. It gives you something to reach for – some intangible fixation that gives you hope each day that you can be just a little bit better.

My friend Jimmy and I were talking about the issue of motivation and he started talking about golf. Usually when Jimmy talks about golf, I stop listening, but today he actually had a point. He told me that there was one significant difference between golf greats David Duval and Tiger Woods. Now, excluding Tiger Woods' personal shenanigans, the primary difference between these two players, says Jimmy, is in their understanding of and pursuit of "mastery" in the game of golf. David Duval's goal was to become the number one ranked player in the world. And he achieved that in April of 1999 – but he hasn't won another tournament since 2001. Now, there are probably a number of contributing factors for his downward spiral, but Jimmy thinks it's because he set a goal, mastered it, and had nowhere to go but down. Perhaps his intrinsic motivation faded. Perhaps he viewed his abilities as finite and he had reached the wall of his ability. So, why bother anymore? A "been-there-done-that-bought-the-t-shirt" mentality is not compatible with continually pursuing an elusive goal.

But, according to Jimmy, Tiger's goal was to become the greatest golfer ever - not just to be ranked as number one. Being the "greatest golfer ever" is an ambition that requires one to continue his engagement. It requires you to constantly chase after the goal and make constant adjustments to either grow closer to the goal or put the goal within reach. But done correctly, you will never reach it – you will always pursue it.

Mastery as an element of intrinsic motivation has the same component – the idea of getting better, chasing the mastery of something but not quite being able to obtain it is a powerful combination for continued motivation. That was the fatal flaw of David Duval's thinking, because according to Daniel Pink, (2009) mastery has three rules: "It requires the capacity to see your abilities not as finite, but as infinitely improvable. Mastery is a pain: It demands effort, grit and deliberate practice. And mastery is an asymptote: It's impossible to fully realize, which makes it simultaneously frustrating and alluring."

3. **Purpose**.

   The third rule is simply "purpose", and for me, this has always been integral to my core thinking and worldview. It's the idea that we as humans, created in the image of God are not placed on this planet randomly. We are designed for purpose and are happier when we pursue purpose.

   Whenever I talk with or work with young people (or people of any age) who haven't figured this out yet, I always see the same patterns. They want to accomplish something, but they're not sure why they want to accomplish it. They haven't made the link between purpose and motivation – and often they get stuck and feel as if they are spinning their wheels. Show me a person who isn't sure what to do and I'll show you a person who hasn't recognized or submitted to the fact that he was designed for something meaningful.

Purpose is a powerful motivating force. Being part of something bigger than yourself lends itself to eternity and reminds you that no matter how long you have on this planet, that what you do may impact lives and linger long after you are gone.

I'll be the first to admit that I love what I do. I love going out into world, seeing the world and telling people about it. It's even more fun when I get to take people with me and show them the world in context. But what motivates me isn't the travel. It's not the sights and sounds. It's the fact that I know there is a broken world out there that needs healing – and peace – and hope. And the idea that God in His sovereignty might use me to bring hope into someone's life is not only humbling; it is compelling.

What motivates me to spend Saturdays teaching workshops or weeks at a time living out of a suitcase or days trying to get a complicated visa sorted out is the fact that I know that I'm connected to something much greater and much more important than me. And there's no amount of money than could motivate me to do these things outside of the fact that I believe it's what I was created to do. That's the power of purpose.

Recap:

1. Studies have shown that there is great intrinsic motivation built into each of us. We are designed to do things for the love of doing them and the satisfaction of accomplishing them.

2. Rewards can sometimes be counterproductive and decrease your intrinsic motivation. In its extreme, we can sometimes trade our freedom for temporary rewards. And without the freedom to choose, we lose motivation and forget our purpose.

3. Conditioning people to respond to a rewards/punishment mentality produces short-term benefits. That's why when people are afraid of losing a job, their performance improves in the short-run. Students who are afraid of failing a class, will study harder – for a while. People who are afraid that they will lose a friend, will be better friends – for a week. But permanent change is different. When people recognize value, when they internally value certain things then behavioral change and motivation are natural results.

4. Three elements that help sustain your intrinsic motivation are: autonomy, mastery and purpose.

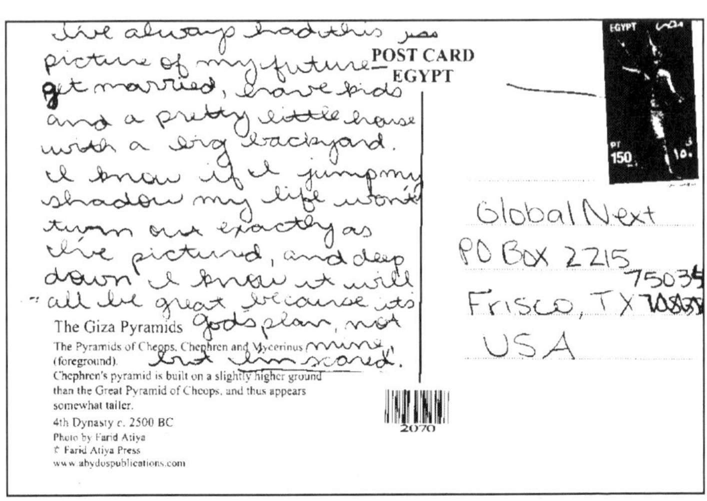

"I've always had this picture of my future – get married, have kids and a pretty little house with a big backyard. I know if I jump my shadow my life won't turn out exactly as I've pictured, and deep down I know it will all be great because it's God's plan, not mine. But <u>I'm scared</u>."

CHAPTER SIX

YOUR JUMP TEAM

CHOOSING THE RIGHT PEOPLE

YOUR JUMP TEAM

Choosing the right people

Jump alone if you must, but not if you don't have to. While choosing to jump is often an individual decision, you can often find others going in the same direction or willing to go in the same direction as you. And if you have the right people and they share similar passions, then tandem-jumping can be personally rewarding and professionally fulfilling. But there are times when you should just jump - with or without anyone.

The Argument for Solo Jumping

There have been times when I've jumped alone and I'm glad I did. I'm happy that I didn't just wait around and do nothing. Jumping alone has its advantages – it's clean, it's based on your timing and you don't have to look after other people. Here are three situations where I think that jumping alone is best:

1. When an idea is new or when you are beginning a brand new project and you need to test out theories or take a test run. You may not want to involve other people until you are certain what you want to accomplish, how you're

going to accomplish it and are able to clearly articulate your goal.

2. When you can conceivably get the job done alone. Why tie up people and their time just for the sake of company. Yes, companionship is great – but you can achieve that in other areas of your life.

3. When you have people who support you, with whom you can toss around ideas, but who you do not need to actually perform any tasks. Sometimes the emotional and intellectual support is enough to allow you to jump alone.

There's another noteworthy component of jumping alone: Lone jumpers take full responsibility for their jumps. In Malcolm Gladwell's (2002) book, *The Tipping Point,* he recounts the case of Kitty Genovese, a young Queens's woman who was attacked by an assailant three times over the course of 30 minutes while 38 of her neighbors watched the horrific event from their windows. No one helped. No one intervened. No one called the police. Most who commented on this tragic event attributed it to the dehumanizing effects of life in large cities. People just didn't want to get involved. But a couple of New York City psychologists, Bibb Latane and John Darley, conducted several experiments that showed that the problem wasn't the apathy of the bystanders. The problem it turns out was that there were *too many* bystanders. Apparently the more people who witness an event, the less likely there are to take personal responsibility for doing anything about it.

In one experiment, Latane and Darley had a student alone in a room fake a seizure. When a student in the next room thought that he or she was the only one to hear the seizure happening, that person came to the aid of the distressed student 85 percent of the time. But when an individual thought there were four other students who also overheard the seizure, they only came to assist the seizing student 31 percent of the time. In a subsequent experiment, people who were alone when seeing smoke coming from under a door reported it 75 percent of the time. When people were in a group, they only reported the potential fire 38 percent of the time. (Gladwell 2002) The researchers concluded that the problem wasn't that people didn't care. The problem was that when there were too many people involved, responsibility became diffused. Everyone thought someone else would take care of the problem.

Imagine that you came upon a horrific car accident and you were the first to arrive on the scene. Of course you'd take out your cell phone and dial 911 and get emergency personnel to respond as quickly as possible. But if you arrived on the scene and saw five other people already there – even if you had no idea when they had arrived – you would assume that someone had already called for help. You would probably do nothing. If there's no one around except for you and the injured person, you will immediately call for help. You *know* it's your responsibility and you take action.

It's the same with jumping alone – if you have a vision and if you recognize an opportunity in this world that's worth jumping for, then you take full responsibility to plan, prepare, calculate and eventually jump. Responsibility does not become spread out. The challenge is clear and you do not wait on others nor do you expect others to take care of the details. And that is one compelling reason to jump alone – you are more likely to take individual responsibility and get things done.

But there is power in community and there is strength in partnership. But it's got to be the right kind of partnership – you must choose the right people.

The Argument for Jumping with Others

People can be complicated and people can get in the way of any opportunity. This is just the truth. At times, people can be the worst. But with the right people working on the right opportunity, for the right reasons, the experience and result can be extraordinary. There is something incredibly satisfying about accomplishing something that matters with a team of like-minded people.

As an American who probably leans heavily on his "individualism," it's important for me (and for people like me) to remember that history is full of examples of teams and fighting forces and groups of people who accomplished incredible things simply because they acted as a team. In their book, *Do Hard Things*, (2008) Brett and Alex Harris mention seventeen-year-old Jeremy Blaschke and how his team decided that they wanted to collect enough money for an ultrasound machine to be used in a crisis pregnancy center. The cost of the machine was $25,000. The aspiration turned out to be a lot harder than Jeremy had imagined. And it took more time than he had hoped. While Jeremy and his team did finally reach and surpass their financial goal, it didn't happen because of a lone person – it happened because of the efforts of the group. Here's how Jeremy describes it: "There's no way I could have done it by myself. I would've gotten frustrated and bored or just burnt-out. They (the team) really gave me the support and encouragement to keep going." (Harris and Harris, 2008)

The following is my short list of when I think you need to assemble a jump team:

1. **When you're ready for something bigger.** Bigger things often require more people. You can't get around this fact. The farther you desire to reach with your jump,

the more people you will need to involve in order to reach your destinations.

2. **When adding people will make you more effective.** No one has all the skills necessary to accomplish everything for every task. Adding people with special abilities will allow you to accomplish things that you could never achieve alone.

3. **When you find the right mix of people that can allow for greater things.** Sometimes the chemistry is just so extraordinary that the whole of the team isn't just greater than the sum of its parts, but exponentially greater.

Choosing the Right People:

Understanding that you will often need other people to accomplish important things is necessary. But you also should make sure you choose the right people for your team. So what should you look for? Each task – each "big life" goal will require something unique, but here are some general qualities you should keep in mind when assembling your team:

1. **Like-mindedness.** You don't have to think exactly like me. You don't have to possess the same style of mental processing that I have. But you'd better care about the same things that I care about if you want to be part of my

team. Jump team members have to have the same core values and want the same outcome in order for the team to function properly.

2. **Passion**. Without passion for the vision of the jump project, you will probably create more problems than you solve and will take more away from the team than you'll give.

3. **Initiative.** I like self-starters. I like people who don't have to be told what to do – people who just do it. In fact, I take note of the time between the germination of an idea and the time it takes a person to actually start making progress on that idea. That tells me just about everything I need to know about how this person will function, work and produce on a team.

4. **Integrity**. If I can't trust you, you have no place jumping with me. Someone who has shady character is the kind of person who might just remove the landing net on the other end of the jump. Not cool. And potentially very dangerous.

My friend Isaac owns a successful technology company. He tells me that trust and honesty are more important to him that a person's skill set. He says he's hired hot shots that have exploited the opportunities he gave them. As Isaac puts it, "Your moral compass is either pointing to the north or to the south. In my experience of working with people, the characteristics of being trustworthy and honest are more valuable to me than someone who says they are the best at something. I can teach team members certain skills that they might not possess. But if they have character and if I cast a vision for them, that will create passion and that will produce better work."

5. **Skill and experience.** While skill and experience may not be more important than integrity, it certainly helps! If your shadow-jumping goal was to build an orphanage in the Sudan, it would be a pretty good idea to have someone on your team who understood the complexities of using a hammer and nails to build something. If you wanted to translate textbooks into a foreign language, put someone on your team who speaks that language! But remember, skills develop and experience grows over time, but I would never trade in character and passion for skill and experience.

6. **Problem-solver.** I love working with people who bring more solutions than problems. Problem-solvers are great team members. They are usually full of great ideas and even if one doesn't work, they have others in the back of

their minds. Problem-solvers tend to make statements like, "How about if we do this…" Or, "Let me figure out a back-up plan and I'll have it for you by tomorrow." God bless problem-solvers!

7. **Available**. Are you free and available to do the job you say you can do? Or will the prospective jump team member agree to be part of your team and then not answer their cell phone, return calls or attend meetings?

   My friend Mohamed Lotfy has worked with teams for international conference events and he also markets and promotes for my company, Global Next, in the Middle East. When I ask him what qualities he most values in team members, he says that what matters most to him are people who are dependable, smart and good problem solvers. But when I ask him what qualities really bug him in a team member he notes a significant frustration when people are too busy to fulfill their commitments.

   And this is a valid point. People often agree to be part of a team without any intention of fulfilling their obligation to the group – or to you as the jump leader. And in my experience, people don't get less busy. It's important to make sure that the people who want to be part of your jump team actually have the time to do the project and to do it well.

Things to Avoid

Just as there are qualities that you look for, there are things that you should avoid when assessing potential jump team members. It would be really easy to make a long list of negative qualities that exist in people. We could just take the opposite of the list I just gave you (people *without* integrity, people who are *not* available, people who are *not* problem-solvers, etc.). But for the sake of time and clarity, I want to focus on just two items. Here are the bright red flags that should tell you who is dangerous and who will probably not help you achieve your jump goals.

1. **People with an agenda.** People do a lot of things for themselves. People tend to look out for their own best interests. Not everyone – but you don't have to look hard to find self-serving people. Avoid them. Eschew their agenda. Recognize it quickly and walk away. People with an agenda are often looking for other people, projects and opportunities to latch on to. And while they look supportive and promising at first, you will quickly find out that they will hijack your vision and move it in their own direction.

   How can you identify people with personalized agendas? First, you'll find them using a lot of personal pronouns, especially words like, "I," "me," and "mine." Listen for this. Most of their conversations will focus on themselves. Second, watch behavior. Actions always speak louder than words and you'd be wise to pay attention to this. When you see self-serving behavior, you should assume that what you're seeing is accurate. When people show you who they are, believe them the first time.

2. **People with a power complex.** If the most important thing to a person is power and position, then they are not qualified to be part of a meaningful jump team. Jumping your shadow, in my philosophy, always has to do with something greater than yourself and bigger than the moment. There is no room for ego. There is no room for political power plays. Don't waste your time playing games.

   A few years ago I partnered with an organization that provides international travel. I agreed to join them to develop their educational programs – which were virtually nonexistent when I arrived. On paper the opportunity looked fantastic. There was challenge, there was purpose and there were important shadows to be jumped. But I soon came to learn that power, control and money were more important to the leaders of the partnering organization than impacting lives and doing things with honor. One of the most valuable lessons I learned during this period of my life was that it is often a waste of time convincing oneself that people are better than they are. I missed the signs of incompatibility mostly because I wanted things to work out, because I could see the potential and that potential was good. But in reality, people who are interested in power and material gain will do whatever is expedient to maintain that status. And that will always be incompatible with those who are jumping for ideas and passions that matter for eternity.

The Ideal Team Makeup

Note the word "ideal." In the real world, we don't often get the "ideal." But still, it's worth pursuing – especially for something as important as your jumps. If I were going to put together an ideal jump team, here are the people who would be on it: (Please note, sometimes one individual can fulfill more than one of these roles at a time. So there's no set number of people you need to have on your team.)

1. **The Kindred Spirit:** This is the person who gets you, who understands you, who shares your passion and who will provide leadership within your jump team. He is the reflection of your passion and dream.

2. **The Glue:** This is your team member who knows people and holds people together. He is probably someone who everyone on your team already knows and respects. He

is also someone who is well connected to the right people outside of your group.

3. **The Charmer:** This is the guy who can convince other people to buy into the message and action of your jump vision. If you teach him to accurately communicate your message, set him loose on the world.

4. **The Information Officer:** This is your go-to person for intelligence. If you need information, if you need to know other specialists, this guy knows all of that information. And if he doesn't know the information, he knows how to find it.

5. **The Bodyguard:** The bodyguard blocks people, issues and distractions from taking you and the team off your track. He doesn't have to look scary or be a muscle bound reptilian. He just has to have the knack of keeping unwanted people and things away from the goal – and sometimes away from you.

6. **The Realist:** This is your team member who basically pokes holes in everyone else's ideas. He's the one who says, "that can't work." And at first you hate him. And if you're not smart, you'll get rid of him. But this guy is the one who kills ideas that can distract you from your purpose.

7. **The Initiator.** The one who will make sure that it gets done. And he'll motivate others to get working and keep them working. This team member knows that talk is cheap – and that if you want to make a difference in this world, things have to get done. And he also knows that sometimes it's smart to jump into the process and figure it out as you go along.

Motivating and Managing your Team

And finally, once you've assembled your team, your focus must turn to motivating your team and keeping them moving forward. And the success of team motivation begins with you – the one with the jump vision.

1. **Be amazing.** It starts with you. If you want your team to be great, you need to be great. Greatness is contagious and attractive. And if you are amazing, you tend to attract higher quality people. As your jump team takes on greatness, then your team attracts others to be a part of your vision or support your message. But it begins with you – are you reflecting and communicating greatness?

2. **Treat your members with respect.** Value people. Find out what makes each member unique and value those qualities. Each person on your team will be different and will bring different things to the table. But while they are different, treat each of them with equal respect. Do not

allow unhealthy competition to emerge that overshadows the purpose of what you, as a team, are trying to accomplish. Do not allow personality conflicts to grow and fracture your group's purpose.

3. **Give team members some freedom.** As I mentioned in our chapter on motivation, autonomy is one of the three factors that helps stoke intrinsic motivation. Give people room to breathe, room to be creative and room to be successful. If you have to babysit people, maybe they shouldn't be on your team. Find people you can trust and give them the independence to do their jobs. Good jump team leaders know that there is a big difference between the appearance of hard work and actual productivity. And often the best ideas happen in spurts – not under the pressure of scrutiny. However, that does not mean that you can disengage. As the team leader, you need to be completely involved, completely aware and ready to gently redirect if things get off course.

4. **Show appreciation to your team.** It doesn't have to be gold watches and caviar. It doesn't need to be new cars and vacation packages. It could be donuts and a trip to the zoo. Whatever it is, show people that you care and that you are interested in investing back into their lives. Let them know they are appreciated and that you recognize what they're doing on behalf of the big picture.

Again, as I have already noted in a previous chapter, people can become de-motivated by rewards. But people are never de-motivated by actions that recognize their worth and reflect your genuine gratitude.

5. **Keep the goal at the forefront.** Never let your team overlook why they're doing what they're doing. You, as the primary jumper, must communicate your vision in such a compelling manner that just the mere mention of the goal is enough to make team members forget petty disagreements and pointless pursuits.

6. **Learn to be quiet.** My wife's uncle, and one of my former college professors, Dr. Sangbok Kim is an extraordinary leader. He has taught thousands of students, founded churches, and served on countless committees for purposes that will only be realized on the other side of eternity. His life represents countless shadows jumped. One time, sitting in his home in Seoul, Korea, I asked him if he could give me one piece of advice regarding team leadership. And he said, "Learn to be quiet and always speak last." He went on to explain that in most meetings everyone's always eager to talk. Some are eager to "prove" themselves and "impress" others. He told me that he had learned how to sit quietly and listen. Really listen. And in the end, he learned more,

understood more and when he finally spoke, he had something worth saying.

Recap:

1. It's better to jump alone than to do nothing.

2. There can be great power and great results when you jump with other like-minded people.

3. Choose your jump team carefully – the people you partner with can make or break you.

4. Stay away from people with personal agendas and power complexes!

5. The success of motivating and managing your jump team is up to you and your choices.

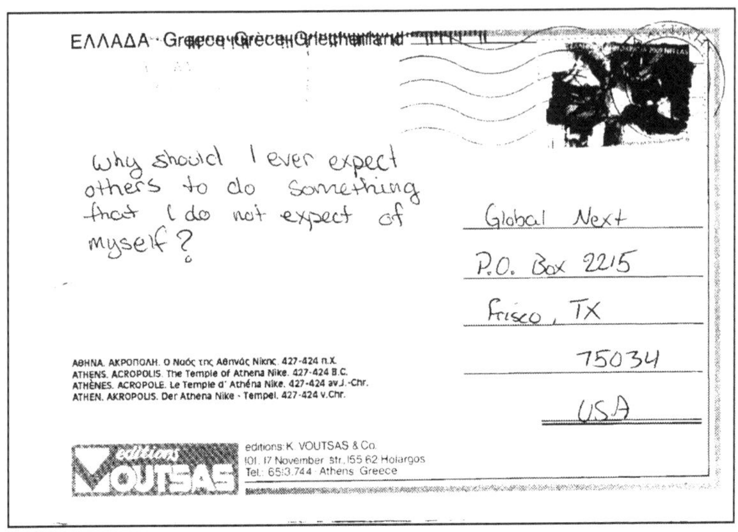

"Why should I ever expect others to do something that I do not expect of myself?"

CHAPTER SEVEN
DREAMING THROUGH THE FINISH

HOW TO DREAM AND GET THE JOB DONE

DREAMING THROUGH THE FINISH

How to dream and get the job done

Dreaming about something and actually doing something are two distinctly different things. Dreaming is fun. Anything is possible in a dream. Things can work out perfectly in a dream – mainly because you don't have to deal with reality, people's weaknesses and global limitations. But you can't stay asleep forever. You can't sleep through shadow jumps.

The Art of Dreaming

The whole point of jumping your shadow is so that you can get beyond your fears, your weaknesses and other obstacles in order to accomplish goals that will influence your life's value and more importantly, impact the world. The goal of a shadow jump is the dream. The value of the dream is often the thing that drives you to jump your shadow. So where do dreams and ideas come from? And how can we learn to stir up our creative juices for more interesting dreams and ideas? Here are ten tips for increasing your creativity:

1. **Read**. Reading leads to ideas. Ideas lead to dreams. Dreams lead to hoping for the world. Hoping for the world leads to doing something about it. Hang out in bookstores and libraries. That's where books live.

2. **Be curious.** Ask people questions. Seek information. Be confused and seek understanding. All of this leads to more creativity. If you go through a day without asking yourself the question "why," "how," or "what if," then you're not living a creative life.

3. **Hang out with interesting people.** Interesting people make you more interesting. My friend Randy used to periodically invite people over to his house – people from diverse backgrounds and with widely varying interests – just to see what would happen. It was often uncomfortable. And awkward. And profitable because it introduced all of us to new people, interesting people and stretched all of our thinking. If you only hang out with people who think exactly like you do, don't complain when you turn out to be boring.

4. **Slow down so that you have time to think.** Sometimes you need to be bored for a bit. And out of boredom creativity can arise- if you let it. We are so afraid of silence and boredom that we will fill our lives with almost any meaningless activity to avoid being alone with ourselves and our thoughts. I have found that when I'm too busy, I don't have time to be creative. When I stop…when I allow myself to slow down…after I've slowed down enough to be bored, my mind starts working and I am more creative.

5. **Go somewhere new.** Once I was scheduled to work in London. I've worked in London a number of times. But I was also working on some writing, and wanted some inspiration. So I looked around and found that I could get a ticket to Stockholm, Sweden for one Euro. (Some ridiculous sale on a European discount airline.) So, I left for London a few days early, flew to Stockholm and sat in a park and wrote. It was glorious. Now, I know, my work tends to lend itself to such locations, but even if it's just a new Starbucks or a new bookstore or a different part of town, the change of scenery will be beneficial. In fact, going to new and faraway places helps with your "psychological distance," which is the next item on the list.

6. **Employ psychological distance.** "It's possible to induce a state of 'psychological distance' simply by changing the way we think about a particular problem, such as attempting to take another person's perspective, or by thinking of the question as if it were unreal and unlikely." (Shapira and Liberman, 2009) The authors of the article, *"An Easy Way to Increase Creativity,"* refer to the work of Lile Jia. In one of his studies, he asked University of Indiana students to list as many different modes of transportation as they could think of. The task was introduced to the participants as having been developed by students studying in Indiana (near

condition) and it was introduced to others as having come from students in Greece (distant condition). Participants who thought the assignment had been developed in Greece were more creative and listed more options. The implication of this study as well as other similar studies by Lile Jia is that you are more creative when you are thinking about faraway places or communicating with people who are dissimilar to us. It increases the likelihood that you'll think differently and therefore be more creative. (Shapira and Liberman, 2009)

7. **Mind Maps.** Mind maps are diagrams that represent your ideas, words, tasks you have to complete and more. Then all of these things are linked together around central ideas or words. They help make good use of lateral, horizontal thinking. It's a good technique for studying and organizing information. Mind Maps are also a useful tool for generating creativity. Start a mind map and you'll be surprised where it will take you!

8. **Take a Media Fast.** You want to start thinking creatively? Get rid of all forms of media from news broadcasts and movies to TV sitcoms and magazines. Get rid of all the things that tell you how to think but actually stifle creativity. Stop being entertained and maybe you'll become more entertaining.

9. **Keep Lists.** Keep a small notebook with you at all times. Put it in your pocket. Keep it under your pillow. Inspiration is a fickle friend – she comes when you least expect her and leaves just as quickly. When she whispers something creative into your ear, you'd be wise to write it down. Oh, and you might want to invest in a pen.

10. **Imagine the Final Destination.** When you attempt to glimpse the end at the beginning it stirs your creativity. Once you start imagining the full version of your dream, your mind immediately goes into problem solving mode. And as you envision the various paths to your success, you will find creativity along the way.

Taking the First Steps

One of the most significant reasons why people don't realize their dreams is because they assume that to accomplish them will take a long time. And as time passes, passion for your dream burns out. Then it's forgotten. Or you're married with five kids. Or you're 103 years old. There are usually three reasons for taking a long time to begin the first steps of a working out a dream: First, you are afraid that the dream will not look as good in reality as it does in your head. Second, you're flat out lazy and can't be bothered to put in the hard work to accomplish your goal. And third, you are such a perfectionist that conditions will never be perfect enough to ensure success. So you keep "researching" and "preparing" and putting off the launch of your idea. But unrealized ideas do not impact a broken world.

In his book, *The Little Big Things: 163 Ways to Pursue Excellence*, Tom Peters (2010) says big results don't necessarily have to take a long time. Here are a few examples Peters shares that illustrate how things can get done quickly:

"The story goes that General George Patton turned around a bedraggled U.S. Army in North Africa in a matter of a few weeks upon taking charge in 1943. (Some say a few days).

Upon taking over a new command, Admiral Lord Nelson would change the attitude of an entire fleet in…less than a week…

A close friend began his teaching career at the age of 40, introduced an entirely new teaching style into a stodgy boarding school…and was voted "top teacher" within ….90 days."

According to Peters, (2010) the bottom line is this: "Change will take precisely as long as you think it will...The arrogance of absurdly high expectations can pay off in very short order if you've got the nerve to go for it and the deep-rooted belief that there's utterly no reason why we can't do this in a month."

So where do you begin? Scott Belsky (2010) says that in order to make ideas happen, there is a simple equation. "Making ideas happen = Ideas + Organization + Communal forces + Leadership capability." In short, if you want to realize your ideas, you've got to start moving in an organized fashion, get the right people on your team and be the right kind of leader.

In his book, *Making Ideas Happen,* Belsky (2010) says every project can be broken down into just three things: "**Action steps** (the specific, concrete things you have to get done), **backburner items** (things that might matter in the future) and **references** (project-related handouts, sketches, notes, meeting minutes that you might want to refer back to later)."

Scott Belsky goes on to tell the story of Chad, an incredibly gifted screenwriter. Film studio heads loved him, but he had trouble getting his genius on paper. He had some success, but more misses than hits. He was also the kind of guy who only checked his email every week or so. No one could get in touch with him and he was extremely disorganized. He was not able to stay on top of his creative ideas and as a result, as brilliant as he was, his dreams were not realized. What he needed was a system – something to bring his chaos, brilliance and ideas into the same room. "A self-proclaimed 'technophobe,' Chad created a paper-based system that displayed the Action Steps for his most important projects in plain sight. He stopped living his life at the mercy of Post-it notes and trying to keep up with e-mail. Instead, he adopted a set of principles and even a few rituals that made him focus on the actionable aspects of his most important projects without abandoning his creative process." (Belsky, 2010)

Once you've organized yourself and have a workable action plan, it's time to turn to your "communal forces." This is what I call your "jump team" as we discussed in chapter six. Great things don't always happen alone. Having the right people around will help you take your dream into reality.

Letting Other People in on the Dream

We take pride in ownership. When it belongs to us, we care more about it. When we build it, we care about it to a ridiculous degree. That's why most of us are so passionate about a dream that we conceive, and construct and invest ourselves in.

But as good as your dream might be, it might be greater if you allow others to become a part of it. If you allow others to dream with you and allow them to take some form of ownership in helping to make the dream work out, then they too will be more passionate about it. But for others to value it, they have to feel as if they have served as co-architect on some aspect of the idea. To understand the pride of creation better, let's take a look at the semi-prepared food industry. There's nothing like a good cake story to help us understand the importance of dream ownership!

When instant baking mixes of all kinds were introduced in the 1940s, not all were received with enthusiasm. Piecrusts and biscuits were acceptable, but housewives resisted instant cake mixes. Why? One theory is that cake mixes simplified the process of baking a cake so much that the housewives didn't feel that the end result was "theirs." Others thought that cakes represented special occasions and that a housewife would be embarrassed to admit that she had made the cake from a "box." The bottom line is that a boxed cake mix took away the pride of creation and the pride of ownership from the baker. As Dan Ariely (2010) describes it in his book *The Upside of Irrationality,* "At the time, a psychologist and marketing expert by the name of Ernest Dichter speculated that leaving out some of the ingredients and allowing women to add them to the mix might resolve the issue. This idea became known as the 'egg theory.' Sure enough, once Pillsbury left out the dried eggs and required woman to add fresh ones, along with milk and oil, to the mix, sales took off."

Evidently, allowing the housewives to increase their personal involved in the "cake mix" process allowed them to view the finished product as more of a reflection of themselves. And you can apply the "egg theory" to including others in your dreams and ideas. Let people add a few "eggs", a little "milk" and some "oil" and watch their interest and enthusiasm grow as they take personal pride and ownership in the creation of something new.

But one warning: Allowing people to be part of your ideas is one thing. Sharing and not being possessive is a great way to get more done. If people wouldn't obsess over personal credit, a lot more could be accomplished. But sharing credit and sharing ownership is not the same as letting someone hijack your dream. If you have an idea that you are passionate about, be vigilant in making sure that it stays on course. Do not confuse sharing with giving it away.

And in the end, regardless as to who's on your jump team, your success will come down to your ability to cast your vision, get other people to buy into it and then lead them to completion. And in order to do that, you have to make sure you don't suffer from one of the most common ailments in the world: procrastination.

Jumping Over Procrastination

I'm sorry, what was that? You'll get to that later? Oh, you have shadows to jump, but you've got some TV to watch, so you'll catch me afterward? Yeah…I've heard that all before. You, sir, are a procrastinator. I've seen your kind before. And yes, I agree, procrastination feels awesome at the time. (Like many unproductive things do.) But you're not helping yourself. And you're definitely not helping the world.

Now, not everyone's an expert procrastinator. If you aren't, then you can skip this section and get back to jumping your shadows. Or maybe you'll read this part anyway, because you've got a friend who needs help. Yeah, that's right - read this for your "friend."

It's not like you plan to procrastinate. And I know that when you do it, you end up feeling guilty about it. You want to stop, but it's become such a habit, you don't know how. Procrastination is the direct enemy of shadow jumping. Procrastination is your comfort zone. And jumping shadows is all about getting past those comfort areas and doing something that matters.

We get away with procrastination because our world allows it. Teachers give students extensions when papers are late. You pay a relatively small late fee when you don't pay your credit card on time. People at work or on your committee will pick up the slack when you fail to perform. And at home, you can just choose not to do things and eventually, someone will sooner or later do what you didn't.

Chronic procrastinators tell themselves lies. They say that they'll feel like doing it tomorrow or that they work better under pressure. They won't and they don't. They will actively seek other activities like checking e-mail and out hanging out on Facebook and assorted other busy-work to help regulate the low level of fear they have about life and possible failure. The biggest lie they tell themselves is that procrastinating doesn't matter - that there are no real consequences. But procrastination has real effects. First, unfinished opportunities are bad for your morale. You want to feel great about yourself? Don't avoid work - finish it. Do something – be somebody. Secondly, procrastination is bad for others. It doesn't just affect you. When things are left to the last minute it creates stress and additional work for everyone around you. And finally, procrastination is bad for your health. Procrastination produces stress, which lowers your immune system, making you more vulnerable to illness and disease. (Marano, 2003)

So, how do you break the habit of procrastination? Here are four suggestions:

1. **Recognize what triggers the habit.** First, admit that you're a procrastinator. Once you own it, you're able to consider what kinds of things you're likely to drag your feet on. School assignments? Work reports? Housework? Keeping up with relationships? Or do you employ procrastination when you feel controlled by others or when you're worried about your performance? Do you procrastinate more when you're tired, angry or nervous? When you begin to recognize the things that bring out your worst procrastination habits, you can prepare, head off the behavior and take a different path. Understanding the pattern reminds you that you have choices. And remember, choices provide freedom.

2. **Redefine yourself**. Start changing the way you think about yourself. Who do you want to be? What do you want to accomplish? If you see yourself as a shadow jumper and someone who wants to pursue a big and meaningful life, you have a greater chance of being that person and putting your life into action. See yourself differently and you will start to behave differently.

3. **Remember: Everything is not a catastrophe.** Jane got a B+ on her report card. It was her first one. She had never received any grade lower than an A before. Immediately she began to think that her dreams of being class valedictorian had slipped away. And without that

feather in her cap, community college loomed in her future. And with a community college education, she would not get a good job, probably become homeless, live in a refrigerator box and sell drugs out of the back flap. Because of a B+. So why try? Why continue? Why not procrastinate? Dr. Monica Basco (2010) says people with catastrophic thinking patterns need to change their focus. If you're afraid of the future, you need to hope for the best but prepare for the worst. Stop scaring yourself and prepare for the most likely (realistic) outcome. And remember how often you've imagined the worst possible outcome and how seldom (if ever) that came to pass. Dr. Basco also encourages people to imagine if a friend found himself in a similar situation. What advice would you give that person? Then, take your own advice.

4. **Learn to prioritize.** Putting first things first is one way to make sure that the most important things don't get left undone. Many people who struggle with procrastination also struggle with organizational skills. Correcting this begins with understanding what's most important and what deserves your focus. Remember, your goal is to complete everything that's important to your day. But feeding your dog is probably more important than online shopping. And tucking in your children at night is definitely more important than updating your Twitter account.

> Some practical ways to deal with this is to make a list of everything that needs to be done during the week. Include deadlines. Put things in order of importance. And don't make it complicated! Limit yourself to no more than five tasks. If you've got more, delete the ones that actually can wait. Don't forget to check items off the list as you finish them. (Basco, 2010) Success breeds success!

Really, when you get down to it, procrastination is all about how you view time – how you value time and what you will do with the time that you have in this life.

The Issue of Time

Time is a funny thing. Time seems to drag by when you're sitting in a boring class or trying to hold your breath for 60 seconds. But when you're hanging out with a fun friend, celebrating a holiday or sleeping, time is fleeting – hard to grasp. Most of us do not keep in the forefront of our minds the actual brevity of life. In comparison with eternity, the seventy or eighty years you have here on earth are really short. It's an incredibly brief amount of time when you subtract the time before you know how to walk, or talk, or feed yourself. And then you have to take out time for showers and eating and other such functions. And take out a few years on the other end when you're too old or senile to make sense. And while you're at it, you might as well deduct time for cutting toenails, eating, watching TV, and laughing politely at your friend's not-so-funny jokes. Wow, when you get down to it, you've only got a few hours left! So what are you going to do with it? In the end, there's never enough of it. In the end, life is always too short to not choose to live it big.

My friend, Michael Nabil, is one of those rare people who know how to "be." He knows how to be "with" you and he knows how to be there "for" you. And once he decided that he and I would be friends that was all there was to it. Every time I came to Cairo to work, he would spend time with me. And we talked about a lot of things for long hours. Michael had reached a point in his life where he knew he wanted to live bigger. But to get the big life he wanted, complete with all of the big impact that comes with that, he knew he was going to have to jump some shadows.

On a visit to Cairo in April of 2010, Michael and I sat and talked. I had brought a book with me to give to him. It was John Piper's book, *Life as a Vapor.* We talked about life and purpose and how short life was when compared to eternity. And Michael told me that he would no longer live a small life – that regardless as to the people he already knew (which were many) and those whom he had already impacted, (which was significant) it wasn't enough. He wanted more. He wanted to jump bigger. And from then on, all I saw in

Michael was expressions and actions of getting out of his comfort zone, jumping his shadow and impacting anyone within his sphere of influence. It's pretty remarkable when you see someone living big and you see the impact of that life playing out in real time.

A few days after I returned home from Egypt, I got a text from my friend Peter telling me that he was sorry, but that Michael had passed away. There were scant details at the time, but Michael's life was indeed a vapor. At the age of 20, he was gone. In an unpleasant ironic twist, the book I had given him had proved prophetic and left in its wake a reminder to all of us, that none of us is guaranteed tomorrow. We don't have time to waste. If we're going to jump, we have only now. There is no value in waiting. You do not know if you'll have another opportunity to jump big or to live big.

Recap

1. Dreaming and talking aren't the same as doing and finishing.

2. To finish anything, you must have an action plan.

3. Let other people in on your dream. Give them some ownership and surround yourself with people who have talents that you might not have.

4. Procrastination is a waste of time.

5. No one is guaranteed tomorrow.

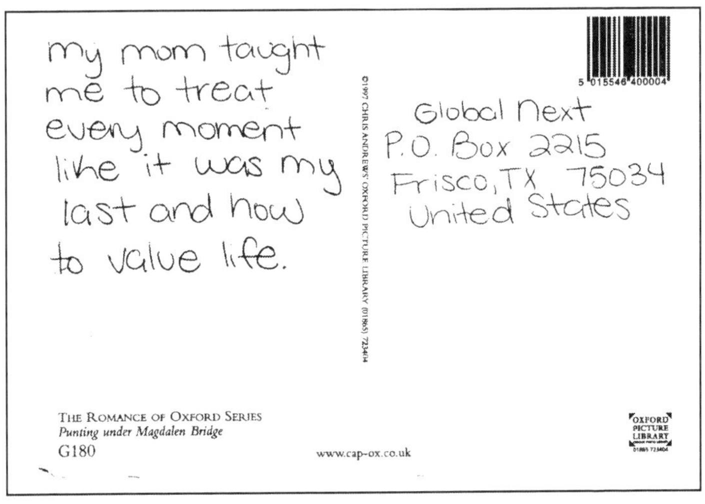

"My mom taught me to treat every moment like it was my last and how to value life."

CHAPTER EIGHT
JUMP HEROES
PEOPLE WHO JUMPED BIG

JUMP HEROES

People who jumped big

Sometimes people live so big that their stories must be told. And as I mentioned in the introduction, good stories have conflict. Without conflict, stories are not gripping. And without stories, life is disconnected and random. Stories give context to life. Stories frame events. At times all we need to motivate us to make a jump is to look at the stories of others who jumped, jumped big, changed themselves, changed others and left the world a little better than they found it. It would be easy to fill a book full of stories of heroes, but for this book I'd like to focus on just four – four people who lived at different times, in different parts of the world and who chose different paths. But they all jumped their shadows for things big and things timeless.

David Livingstone

Through Global Next's Leadership Conference division, I take students to England where for one of our learning activities, we visit Westminster Abbey. The primary reason I take them to this magnificent church is to see the burial place of David Livingstone and to talk about his life. Livingstone was born March 19, 1813 in Scotland to a poor family. At the age of 10 David had to take a full-time job in a textile factory working 14 hours a day. He studied at night and through the weekends. But David Livingstone didn't think of himself as a victim. He simply did what he had to do to live the big life he believed that God had for him. He received his medical degree in 1940 and by 1941 had made his jump to Africa – and this is where his legacy took hold. Before Livingstone, Africa's interior was almost entirely unknown to the rest of the world. Livingstone lived what I like to call the trilogy of a purposeful life: Going, Bringing and Leaving. (More specifically: Going into the world, bringing hope to the world and leaving things better than you found them.)

Going: David Livingstone was able to see the world outside of his comfort zone in Scotland. He yearned for an opportunity to see and explore God's world at a time when few men would have bothered. He understood that sometimes a person makes a difference where he is and that other times the world in need is only a 98-day boat ride away. And when it is, you jump your shadow and chase your purpose. (And to think that we complain of plane rides of 8 hours!)

With his interest in exploration, Livingstone crossed the continent of Africa, survived an encounter with a lion and discovered what is now known as Victoria Falls, the source of the Nile River. Because of his jump, he captured the imagination of the world. He inspired others to see things beyond their borders.

Bringing Hope: The second part of his trilogy was his purpose. Livingstone's faith in God was so strong and so central to his life that he could not imagine being anywhere without sharing the hope of heaven that could be found through faith in Jesus. And he shared that with the indigenous people of Africa, changing their lives and giving them hope and purpose.

Leaving Things Better: Finally, he recognized the injustice of the slave trade of East Africa and endeavored to expose it and do something about it. In fact, Livingstone viewed his work in this area as much more significant than his discovery of the source of the Nile as evidenced by a letter he wrote to the New York Herald:

"And if my disclosures regarding the terrible Ujijian slavery should lead to the suppression of the East Coast slave trade, I shall regard that as a greater matter by far than the discovery of all the Nile sources together." — Livingstone in a letter to the editor of the New York Herald. (1871)

I guess one of the things I really admire about David Livingstone is that he didn't just sit at home and pray. He didn't just send a check. He didn't just read the daily newspaper and click his tongue at the injustices in the world. He got up, and went, and involved himself in something he believed in. He jumped shadows that most of will never have in front of us. And in so doing, he left behind the fingerprints of his soul. His grave marker gives testimony to all of this:

Brought by Faithful Hands Over Land and Sea
Here Rests David Livingstone:
Missionary Traveler Philanthropist
For Thirty Years His Life was Spent in an Unwearied Effort To Evangelize the Native Races To Explore the Undiscovered Secrets
To Abolish the Devastating Slave Trade of Central Africa
Where With His Last Words He Wrote:
"All I can add in my solitude is: May heaven's rich blessing come down On everyone, American, English or Turk Who will help to heal this open sore of the world."

His words were true then and they are true today. We need healing for the open sores of the world. We need people who are willing to get past their misconceptions, past their fears and past their addiction to comfort and bring hope to a world that is broken and whose condition is that of an open, gaping wound.

Enduring Jump Legacy: Livingstone's legacy rests in how he opened the world to possibilities beyond their borders. His example of a jump made others realize that it was possible for them to jump too. It wouldn't be easy, but it could be done. And suddenly the world was a lot bigger for so many people.

Dietrich Bonhoeffer

Have you ever been confronted with evil? Have you ever recognized your moment to impact the world and had to decide if you would jump your shadow or not? Have you ever considered giving your life for a cause greater than yourself? Dietrich Bonhoeffer did. He was a Lutheran pastor during World War 2. In addition, he was a participant in a resistance movement against Nazism. He also lost his life because of the shadow he jumped.

In 1938 Bonhoeffer, living in Germany, made his first contact with members of the German Resistance. But by 1939, Bonhoeffer had decided to go to America. He was concerned about fighting in the war in Europe. He was even more concerned about pledging an oath to Hitler. At the time, he wasn't willing to accept the coming conflict in his life, so he left and went to a place where he thought he would be safer. Where he thought life would be more predictable and difficult decisions wouldn't haunt him.

But when you're born for something greater than yourself, your soul will not let you rest, nor will it allow you take the easy way out. Here is one way Bonhoeffer characterized his decision to jump his shadow: "If I see a madman driving a car into a group of innocent bystanders, then I cannot, as a Christian, simply wait for the catastrophe and then comfort the wounded and bury the dead. I must try to wrest the steering wheel out of the hands of the driver." (Bethge, 2000)

Soon, Bonhoeffer made the decision to go back to Germany. Here's what he wrote to Reinhold Niebuhr: "I have come to the conclusion that I made a mistake in coming to America. I must live through this difficult period in our national history with the people of Germany. I will have no right to participate in the reconstruction of Christian life in Germany after the war if I do not share the trials of this time with my people... Christians in Germany will have to face the terrible alternative of either willing the defeat of their nation in order that Christian civilization may survive or willing the victory of their nation and thereby destroying civilization. I know which of these alternatives I must choose but I cannot make that choice from security." (Bethge, 2000)

In 1940, Bonhoeffer joined the Abwehr, a German intelligence organization. The organization also happened to be the center of the anti-Hitler resistance. From his involvement in German intelligence, Bonhoeffer became aware of the full extent of the Nazi atrocities. Under the cover of the Abwehr, he served as a courier for the German resistance movement using his global contacts to advance the international understanding of resistance movements inside of Germany and to enlist the support of Allied nations in post-war negotiations.

On April 6, 1943, Bonhoeffer was arrested when documents were discovered that linked him to the anti-Hitler conspiracy. And while Bonhoeffer was successful in explaining away the appearance of a connection between him and the anti-Hitler conspiracy, he was nevertheless sent to prison for other charges including subverting Nazi policy toward the Jews and misusing his position in the Abwehr to further his church work.

But even while in prison, Bonhoeffer continued to use his life of purpose by attempting to bring hope to fellow prisoners and through his writings, which were smuggled out of prison and later published, continuing his legacy, long after his life ended.

After the July 20 plot on Hitler's life in 1944 failed, a definitive link was finally made between Bonhoeffer and the conspirators. On April 9, 1945, just a month before the Nazi regime would surrender, Bonhoeffer was executed. The camp doctor who witnessed the execution wrote: "I saw Pastor Bonhoeffer ... kneeling on the floor praying fervently to God. I was most deeply moved by the way this lovable man prayed, so devout and so certain that God heard his prayer. At the place of execution, he again said a short prayer and then climbed the few steps to the gallows, brave and composed. His death ensued after a few seconds. In the almost fifty years that I worked as a doctor, I have hardly ever seen a man die so entirely submissive to the will of God." (Bethge, 2000)

No one ever said you were going to get out of this life alive. Sometimes to jump your shadow means making the ultimate sacrifice. But most of us haven't yet figured out what to live for, much less what or who we'd die for.

Enduring Jump Legacy: Bonhoeffer left a legacy through his life and through his writings. His jump forced others to realize that when evil exists, when evil is rampant, you cannot sit by and do nothing. You can't wish it away – you have to stand against it at all costs. Even at the cost of your life.

Abdul Sattar Edhi

Richard Covington, in his aptly entitled article *"What One Person Can Do,"* (2008) tells the amazing account of Abdul Sattar Edhi. The impact of this man's life is astonishing. His organization, the Edhi Foundation "shelters and counsels battered wives, rescues accident victims, feeds poor children, houses homeless families, cares for the mentally incompetent and buries unclaimed corpses." (Covington, 2008) In short, this man takes care of everyone and everything that most people wouldn't touch with a ten-foot pole.

Abdul Edhi, a devout Muslim, has chosen to jump shadows. He didn't wait until he had amassed a complete education. He didn't depend upon governments and organizations before he chose to jump. He recognized the broken world around him and he gave his life in service to help those who couldn't help themselves. According to Covington's article:

1. He has only a primary-school education.

2. He refuses to accept any financial help from the Pakistani government.

3. He won't accept financial help from any organized religion.

4. Edhi explains his philosophy on fund-raising like this: "I tell people that, because I am working for you, the money must come from you."

5. He's created one of the largest and most successful health and welfare networks in Asia.

6. His small staff and more than 7,000 volunteers help tens of thousands of Pakistanis every day.

Remarkably, his work reaches beyond the borders of Pakistan. His organization has delivered medical supplies, food and clothes to places like Bosnia, Ethiopia and Afghanistan. After the 9/11 attacks Edhi donated $100,000 to Pakistanis in New York City who had lost their jobs as a result of the attacks.

Abdul was born in 1928 in a small town north of Mumbai. His father made a decent living in textiles. But from his childhood his parents impressed upon him the importance of living simply and of giving to others. "Every day before school, my mother would give me two *paisa* and say, 'Spend one *paisa* on yourself and give the other away.' When I came home, she would ask me where I had given away my one *paisa*. It was her way of creating an awareness in me of the need for social welfare." (Covington, 2008)

Abdul Edhi, now well into his eighties, shows no signs of slowing down. He's decided to make his life about others. He's motivated the masses to give to his vision, so that thousands of lives are changed. As one person who chose to jump, the world is a little easier for many.

Enduring Jump Legacy: If you live your vision in a compelling way, people will respond. You don't have to compromise and sell your soul to achieve your jump and realize your dreams. And your single choice can move the world.

John from the Sudan

The final story is about a young man named John. You probably don't know his story. I didn't know his story until my friend Vernon told it to me. John didn't cure cancer or discover a new planet. He didn't make his first million before he was thirty or have a hand in the invention of the Internet. He didn't live big in the way most of the Western world measures bigness. But in God's economy he lived big.

First, let me tell you about Vernon. Among other things, Vernon Burger is the founder and executive director of His Voice for Sudan (www.hisvoiceforsudan.com). There are two things I know for sure about Vernon. He cares about truth and he cares about people. He says that God gave him a heart for orphans and widows and he spends his time jumping his shadow to do things that will never make him rich and will never make him famous. He jumps his shadow so that he can build orphanages and schools in southern Sudan. But Vernon doesn't seem to be the kind of guy who spends a lot of time talking about himself. He is more interested in investing in other people's lives and telling the stories of others. And that's how I heard about John. Here's how Vernon tells the story:

"Here's an example of someone who isn't controlled by their past. We have an orphan in the Sudan by the name of John. He's 13 years old. A couple of years ago he was walking and heard the most feared noise in Sudan – a hissing sound followed by an explosion. That's the sound of tripping a landmine. It blew off both of his legs. It blew off his lip and he was laying there bleeding to death. Some people come and they take him back to his parents. What do his parents say? 'You are an ugly disgrace. Get out.'
It makes you wonder which pain was worse… losing his legs or being rejected by his parents? Don't wonder too long, it was the second one – the pain of rejection.

Yet here's what John did. He came to the orphanage and we fitted him for prosthetic legs and it turns out that he is the most brilliant kid out of all three of the schools we have in the Sudan. He's top of the class. And because he is constantly resting in the loving kindness of God who has healed the pain of the rejection of his parents, he goes out and mentors other kids in the school and disciples them.

Three months ago, John was our first orphan to die. He got a case of incurable malaria and within 2 days he was dead. Just gone. And here's the question: In John's short life, did he finish strong as a 13-year-old? He did…he was able to finish strong because he wasn't controlled by his past. His pain didn't control him. He let Christ heal it…"

And that's the remarkable thing about John. He understood pain, physical and emotional pain, but he wasn't controlled by it. Because of the healing power of Christ in his life, he was able to jump his shadow and invest his life in others. Though many would view John as broken, John didn't view himself as exempt from the responsibility of reaching out to the broken world around him. He did not define himself by his pain. He defined himself by his relationship with God and the hope that anchored his soul.

Enduring Jump Legacy: It doesn't matter where you are, or what's happened to you. You can jump, love and impact those in your world. You are more than your pain. Your past does not need to define you.

Recap:

1. People can make a difference, individually and collectively.

2. People never make a difference by staying in their comfort zones.

3. Do not let your past or your pain define you.

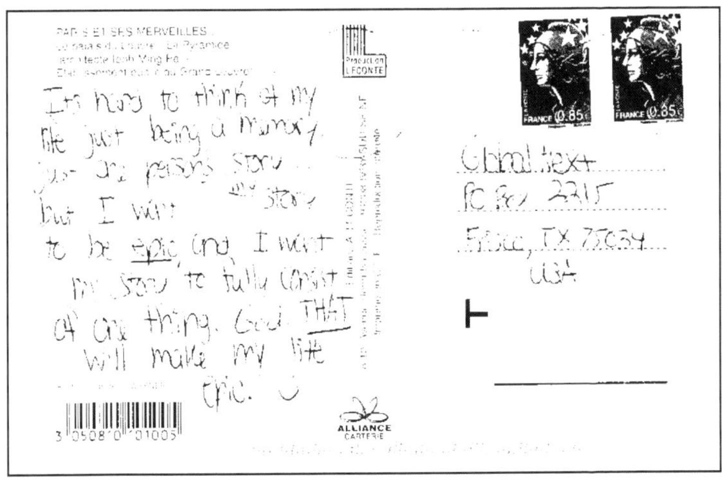

"It's hard to think of my life just being a memory. Just one person's story... but I want my story to be <u>epic</u> and I want my story to fully consist of one thing: God. <u>THAT</u> will make my life epic."

CHAPTER NINE
THE REBOUND
GETTING UP AFTER FALLING

THE REBOUND
Getting up after falling

You will fall. I just want to say that up front. If you jump, you will fall. You cannot live the life of a jumper and not occasionally experience the unpleasant effects of gravity. Sometimes it's because of things beyond your control. Sometimes it's because you simply didn't do things right. You made mistakes or you didn't prepare. It's going to happen. We are bound by our humanity and will continue to be less than perfect. I am more interested in how to handle falling and failure than in debating when or why it's going to happen. And actually, I don't have a whole lot to say on this issue. To me it's pretty simple: First, you don't always get what you want. Second, sometimes things don't work out the way you thought it would. Third, guard yourself against bitterness and resentment. Fourth, if you fall because of your failures or your mistakes, make things as right as you can and limp along. And fifth, pick yourself up and jump again. That's pretty much it. Let me explain…

You Don't Always Get What You Want

I wanted to see what was going on in Gaza for myself. The war, dubbed Operation Cast Lead by Israel and Massacre of Black Saturday by Hamas, was a three-week event in the winter of 2008-2009. Gaza and Israel is a complicated issue

– one that will not be solved in this book. From the Israeli view, they disengaged from Gaza at the insistence of the global community in 2005 and left this tiny strip of land to the self-rule of the Palestinians. In 2006, Palestinians in Gaza elected Hamas as their democratically elected leaders. Weary of dealing with rockets and mortars coming from Gaza into Israeli civilian territory, the IDF took action in 2008 inside Gaza – significant action. From the Hamas viewpoint, Israel is an illegal occupier of any part of Palestine and they will not give up fighting until all of their land has been restored to them. But I like to see things for myself and talk to people myself to try to make sense of situations that are rarely as simple as the media likes to portray them.

I have two contacts inside Gaza that were waiting to meet me on the other side of the border. They had agreed to show me around, give me their perspective and introduce me to others. But I couldn't get in. I went to the border. I spoke to the authorities there. They said no. I called people. And then I called other people. After a couple of hours of banging my head against the door to Gaza, I had no choice but to give up. I hate to give up on something I want. I wanted to see for myself what was going on. I wanted to talk to people and see what life was like inside of this region and what the average person thought about Hamas, their tactics and their goals, what they thought about the Israelis, who had lost who in this battle where so many civilians were killed. But I couldn't. And I didn't.

Sometimes you might want a certain jump and you just can't get a launching pad no matter what you do. Then I got a phone call from one of my sources inside Gaza. They told me not to try to come that day (as if I had a choice!) because more than one hundred people had been killed on the streets of Gaza City in a standoff between Hamas and rogue gangs. It happened in the very place I was headed. And this is when I realized that sometimes you might have the desire to jump and sometimes God grounds you. And you pick yourself up, find another direction and continue. Sometimes it's just wrong timing. Sometimes it's just not what you need to be doing. And you don't have to determine which of those it is at that moment. The lesson: You don't always get what you want, but you do not have permission to get discouraged and give up.

Things Don't Always Work Out the Way You Thought They Would

Everyone experiences frustration when we don't get what we want. Sometimes it's not a mistake, the results are just unexpected. I expected that I could meet my contacts inside Gaza. I couldn't. I also expected to achieve my interview with a Hamas official the first time I went to Syria. In reality, it took two years of building trust and finding the right time to achieve that jump goal.

And sometimes you jump and land somewhere unexpected and uncomfortable and things are not at all the way you thought they would be. I experienced this when I jumped from Florida to Texas. I had made a tough decision to jump my shadow, take a risk, drag my family across the country, leave a good job in pursuit of what I thought would be an amazing opportunity. It wasn't. When I arrived in Texas to partner with a travel organization and provide them with access to my leadership programs, I had hopes as high as any I've ever had in life. And within a very short period of time, I found myself very disappointed. Over the next four years, I would become frustrated with organizational dishonesty, disillusioned with people whom I had trusted and annoyed that God had brought me here.

As I look back, (and time is always a great perspective setter) I can see more clearly that this jump was important. While it didn't turn out as I had expected, and while I was personally disappointed in the character of the people I found myself with, God had a purpose for it. The experience prepared me for the next jump and for what I am doing today - and I wouldn't want to miss where I am now for anything. Here's what I learned from that particular period:

1. People are not better than you think they are. I don't mean that in a cynical way – and I sort of hope I'm wrong. But experience is not on the side of hope in this situation. At least not more than 10 percent of the time. But I find that often we make excuses for people's bad behavior at the expense of seeing the truth and dealing with the circumstances as they present themselves.

2. Do not depend upon people; keep your focus on God, who never changes. Don't lose the focus of God's plan for you in the middle of frustration.

3. Accept that change is inevitable. The more you embrace the possibility of change, the better prepared you will be when it inevitably comes knocking on your door.

4. Don't let others and their unwise, unethical choices, define you. If that means walking away from a situation, an opportunity or a job, walk away.

5. Get over things quickly. There is no value in holding on to offenses and grudges. They are always counter-productive.

And that brings me to my next point…bitterness.

Don't Get Bitter

One of the biggest dangers of disappointing jumps is that you might get bitter and allow resentment to flourish. Bitterness is one of those emotions that has surprisingly deep roots. When we allow ourselves to hold on to bitterness, to become resentful, we abandon control of our future. We limit our choices.

David Jeremiah writes about the power of resentment in his book, *Slaying the Giants in Your Life* (2001). "When we opt to cling to bitterness, it's as if we've placed ourselves under an evil spell. Only the ancient and godly remedy of forgiveness will remove that spell." Jeremiah goes on to discuss the classic book *Forgive and Forget* by Lewis Smedes. In his book Smedes recounts a play that illustrates how powerful resentment and bitterness can be.

The play is about a German general and a French journalist. The general, Herman Engel, has been sentenced to 30 years in prison because of his crimes during World War 2. But the journalist, Morrieaux, is furious. His entire family was massacred by Engel's troops and prison is not enough justice for the journalist. He wants Engel to pay with his life. Over the years, Morrieaux becomes obsessed with Engle and his fate. Years later, when Engel is released from prison as an old and broken man, he and his wife desire nothing more than to live out their days in anonymity. They build a cabin in the woods near Alsace. What he doesn't know is that Morrieaux has been following his every move. Morrieaux goes to the nearby town and stirs up hatred for the old general. He convinces the villagers to rise up and take revenge on the old general. The plan is to burn the general's cabin and shoot him and his wife.

But the journalistic instincts of Morrieaux get the best of him. Before the plan can be enacted, Morrieaux pays a visit to Engel at his cabin in the woods. He wants more details about what had happened during the massacre all those years ago and what had happened to his family. What he doesn't expect is to find an old man who looks like anything but a monster. The old general struggles to recall even the smallest of details from the past. And Morrieaux finds himself not nearly as angry as he thought he would be.

As David Jeremiah tells it, "Suddenly Morrieaux blurts out all the mob's plans for the next day, he offers to lead them out of the woods and save their lives. Engel listens and replies, 'I'll go with you – on one condition. I'll go with you if you'll forgive me.'

Morrieaux hesitates. This is a difficult question for a man who has built his entire life around the hope of destroying his adversary. He has killed the old German in his heart many times over three decades. Amazingly, Morrieaux discovers that he's perfectly capable of rescuing his old enemy; he's more than willing to call off the execution.

But forgive him? That he cannot do.

The Engels don't leave. And the next evening, they die at the hands of the rabid mob." (Jeremiah, 2001)

And that is the destructive power of bitterness. Morrieaux spent his entire life dedicated to hating a man and missing the opportunities in his own life. In the end he found that he could rescue with his hands, but could not forgive with his heart. And it's just not worth it to allow someone…anyone to occupy so much space in your head and heart. If you live at all, you will get hurt. You will be disappointed. But holding on to it only diminishes your future – it only restricts your jumps and it becomes a shadow of immeasurable proportions ever more difficult to jump.

What if You Mess Up?

You will. You will disappoint someone. You will not do what you promised. You will not do your best. You will walk away from something and someone and will probably regret it. What should you do when you mess up?

1. When you mess up, admit it. Don't pretend it didn't happen. Don't twist the facts. Don't rationalize. Don't justify. Just own it and take responsibility for it.

2. Once you recognize the mistake and take responsibility for it, do your best to make things right. This might include an apology and it might include correcting whatever you can to make things right.

3. Accept the consequences that come with making mistakes. This is the hardest part. Opportunities can be lost. Relationships might be fractured. Trust can be destroyed. Some things can't be undone.

4. Don't keep making the same mistakes. Learn from your mistakes. If you fail to learn...if you refuse to follow through on commitments, continually miss meetings, fail to return phone calls or emails, produce mediocre work, or worse, choose to be dishonest, cheat or stab others in the back, then you've got more shadows to jump than simple fear and normal challenges. You've got the worst version of yourself to jump. And at some point, that might be a bigger jump than you can make.

Pick Yourself Up and Jump Again

None of us likes failure, disappointment or messing up. We don't like negative experiences. It affects us and affects how we feel about jumping. In the psychological world this is called "negativity bias." As Jonathan Haidt (2006) puts it, "In marital interactions, it takes at least five good or constructive actions to make up for the damage done by one critical or destructive act. In financial transactions and gambles, the pleasure of gaining a certain amount of money is smaller than the pain of losing the same amount. In evaluating a person's character, people estimate that it would take twenty-five acts of life-saving heroism to make up for one act of murder." So, I get that negative experiences are more powerful than positive ones. I understand that any negative experience you have in a jump attempt is likely to outweigh any positive experience you have. And that's because it's much easier to scare your Elephant (emotions) than to engage your Rider (intellect).

But let me appeal to the truth. We need to realize that sometimes when we experience failure in the short term it produces something far greater for the long run. Sometimes experiencing failure produces character and determination that helps you develop into a person who can jump higher and longer. But that depends on you and how you ultimately respond to the struggles that are a part of life. In the end, you will experience success in jumping your shadow not because you'll never fail, but because you'll get back up and jump again.

Recap

1. If you take big risks, you will experience disappointment and failure from time to time: Expect it.

2. Never let bitterness take root – it will cost you more than it will cost anyone else.

3. Learn to get over things. Perspective is your choice.

4. When you fall, when you fail, get up and jump again.

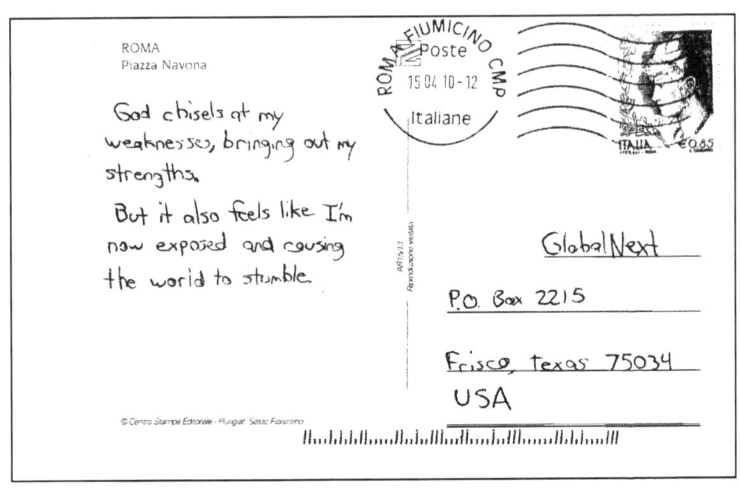
ROMA
Piazza Navona

God chisels at my weaknesses, bringing out my strengths.

But it also feels like I'm now exposed and causing the world to stumble.

ROMA FIUMICINO CMP
Poste Italiane
15.04.10 - 12

ITALIA €0,65

GlobalNext
P.O. Box 2215
Frisco, Texas 75034
USA

AR15/13
Riproduzione vietata

© Centro Stampa Editoriale - Plurigraf Sesto Fiorentino

"God chisels at my weaknesses, bringing out my strengths. But it also feels like I'm now exposed and causing the world to stumble."

CHAPTER TEN
THE ARTICLES
EVIDENCE OF A JUMP

THE ARTICLES

Evidence of a jump

So, here we are at the end of this book. Part motivation, part strategy and part personal narrative. It's all in there. And now at the end, I will include some of the articles I've written about some of the jumps I've made.

I'm not finished jumping and in many ways, I feel like I'm just beginning, but the following are part of what I've done once I started thinking bigger – once I chose to get out of my comfort zone and be part of something bigger than myself.

And while it's not always easy – I've loved my jumps. Jumping to Florida to develop educational programs for a large organization led me to what I do today. Jumping to Texas to partner with an organization that ended up being a nightmare still taught me how to endure, forced me to jump bigger and fortunately, opened up new doors and new passions for me.

Working in the Middle East is no picnic either, but I wouldn't change it for the world. The people I've met have enriched my life, forced me to be more patient, broken my heart for things that matter and have woven their lives into mine – some more deeply than others.

The following are some articles written from that region of the world – whether or not you find the information interesting or not or even agree with the information is not nearly as important as understanding that they are the product of jumping. They are laced with meaning, being and purpose. As you read them, you'll find mostly just the facts – there wouldn't be room enough in this book to talk about the personal impact, the shoulders that have been rubbed, and the hearts that have been changed. No, that will have to wait for a few more jumps before those stories are told.

Temples, Arks and Heifers

An Interview with the Temple Institute of Jerusalem

Phil Johnson, Ph.D.
From Jerusalem
Original interview 2007 / Updated in 2010

Great. This was going to require a supervisor. The security officers at El Al, Israel's notoriously thorough airline are very good at their jobs and not always easy to deal with. Earlier that late March morning in 2007 my flight to Israel had been canceled and I had been rebooked on El Al Airlines and the security officers were not happy that I had made the sudden switch. Neither were they happy that my passport revealed recent trips to Egypt, Morocco and Istanbul. And they definitely were not happy about the letters I was carrying in my carry-on bag. The documents were really just printouts from the website of the Temple Institute, the organization I had spent the last two and a half months trying to arrange an interview with; the reason for my visit to Israel. The letters I was carrying were written in Hebrew and translated into English. They represented correspondence from the Temple Institute to the police department in Jerusalem complaining about the treatment religious Jews had received when attempting to visit the Temple Mount. For some, the Temple Institute is a controversial organization. The Temple Mount in Jerusalem is a controversial bit of real estate. And now I was controversial enough to be escorted to the "little room" for further investigation. I asked the investigating agent what it was exactly that made me appear so suspicious. He looked at me with just a touch of humor in his eyes and said, "I could tell you, but then I'd have to kill you." Then his gaze hardened and he whispered, "Seriously, if you want to know what I know about you, then apply for my job." I wasn't sure I wanted to know that much about myself, so I decided that for the time being I would not submit my application for employment.

Finally, after a thorough interrogation, I was allowed to board the plane and several hours later I arrived in Tel Aviv. Of course after standing at baggage claim for 45 minutes I realized that my suitcase was not going to arrive. Evidently

El Al's security folk decided that it was best for my luggage and me not to travel together. No matter, while I waited, I made contact by cell phone with Mr. Yitzchak Reuven, the assistant director of the International Department of the Temple Institute. For months he had been hesitant to meet with me and even my arrival in Israel was no guarantee that we would meet. But after speaking on the phone this time, even with his obvious hesitation, he finally agreed to meet and allow me to conduct an interview. We agreed on a time and place and I was ready to get to my hotel and get some sleep. I headed out of the airport looking for a taxi. The Nesher van taxis are the cheapest. They will take you right to your hotel in Jerusalem for a modest fee. The catch is you have to wait a little while for them to fill up with other passengers. Of course when one waits in Israel, lots of things can happen.

The last time I landed in Israel in the summer of 2006 the military engagement in the Gaza Strip had just begun, which turned out to be a prelude to the 2nd war with Lebanon. This time my waiting was interrupted by a swarm of police vehicles and the closing of the entire Ben Gurion airport. A young man was perched on the ledge of the parking garage threatening to jump. Afraid that he might have explosives strapped to his chest the police officers began shouting for everyone to get back inside the airport. This is when I learned that the Nesher taxis will leave the airport even when they are not full. The combination of offering the driver more money and the prospect of spending the night in the airport proved to be the perfect motivation for departing the airport quickly. As we rapidly headed away from the airport and towards Jerusalem, I was reminded of how unpredictable this world is and how volatile this particular corner of the world has always been. Jerusalem, the Holy City, is the most disputed piece of real estate on the planet. Sacred to Christians, Jews and Muslims, this city holds captive the collective imagination of the world. And now I had come to see what I could find out about the activities and thinking of the Temple Institute. I wanted to know what this organization knew about this piece of property and about their ambitious plans to reconstruct the Temple of Jerusalem. I had questions that I hoped they could answer.

The Temple Institute

According to the Temple Institute's website, the Institute is, "dedicated to every aspect of the concept of the Holy Temple of Jerusalem, and the central role it fulfilled, and will once again fulfill, in the spiritual well being of both Israel and all the nations of the world." (www.templeinstitute.org) According to the site, the

Institute's work includes helping others to understand the Temple's past, present and future. This includes education, research, and development. One of the Institute's ultimate goals is to see the Temple rebuilt on Mount Moriah in Jerusalem according to biblical commandments.

As part of their educational goals, the Temple Institute runs a small museum located at 19 Misgav Ladach Street called *Treasures of the Temple.* The museum is filled with vessels and instruments that have been created by accomplished craftsmen for use in the future Holy Temple. Each of these items, which include the altar, the laver, the menorah, table of showbread and priestly garments, has been recreated according to exact biblical requirements. The museum also offers an audio-visual presentation, a look at a scale model of the Second Temple, guided tours and a variety of publications and educational materials.

The Temple Institute's literature reveals that the Institute is also involved in the production of a Red Heifer, a sacrificial animal necessary for temple worship to resume. And the Institute claims to know the exact location of the Ark of the Covenant. All of this was enough to pique my interests and cause me to want to know more about this organization, their plans and how they believed these plans might play into God's ultimate design for humanity.

Temple Denial

Of course, talk of building a Jewish Temple on the very location that currently hosts the Dome of the Rock, Islam's third most holy site, seems rather absurd in today's complicated geopolitical climate. It is not likely that Muslims will ever willingly welcome a Jewish presence on the Temple Mount and in fact, the climate indicates that Palestinian Muslims are more in favor of completely denying that the Jews ever had a historic presence in Israel.

In his book, *The Fight for Jerusalem*, Dore Gold discusses how the Palestinian/Islamic battle for Jerusalem incorporates more than just the military assault of the intifada. Gold states, "Its first stages entailed a campaign by Arafat to completely delegitimize the Israeli claim to the city. This began on the ninth day of the Camp David summit, when Yasser Arafat subjected Clinton to a lecture of staggering historical revisionism. His central argument was that the biblical temples never existed on the Temple Mount or even in Jerusalem. Arafat baldly asserted that 'There is nothing there [i.e. no trace of a temple on the Temple Mount],' further insisting that 'Solomon's Temple was not in Jerusalem, but Nablus.'" (Gold, 2007)

Gold goes on to say that this sort of statement caused Arafat to lose credibility in the West, but that his doctrine of "Temple Denial" caught fire with Palestinians and gained credibility even among Western-educated Palestinians. Even

Arafat's successor, Mahmoud Abbas, who is generally viewed by the West as more moderate than his predecessor, embraces Temple Denial as much as Arafat and others in the PLO leadership.

From Dore Gold's perspective, once Yasser Arafat had "moved the goalposts of historical truth," (Gold, 2007) it wasn't long before this revision of history was embraced by Islamic universities around the world. This is reflected in the claims of Jordanian lecturers, who with the backing of German scholars state that David and Solomon were simply fictional characters. And to impact the thinking of future generations of Islamic students even more, a history lecturer at Saudi Arabia's Muhammad bin Saud Islamic University published research indicating that King Solomon's Temple was in fact a mosque. (Reiter, 2005)

In addition, according to the *Jerusalem Post*, a bulldozer is now a common feature on the Temple Mount "ripping up earth on the Temple Mount, at the Dome of the Rock platform," and in the process destroying valuable archaeological finds related to Jewish history on the Mount. Most likely fearing the disturbance of the fragile and volatile relationship between Jews and Palestinians, the Israel Antiquities Authority has maintained a hands-off position according to the article. (*Jerusalem Post*, July 14, 2007)

Clearly, from a human perspective, the current environment is not conducive to the building a third Temple on this spot!

Current Events and Prophecy

An additional element that makes the efforts of the Temple Institute so intriguing is the connection that some have noted between the Temple Institute's efforts, current events and biblical prophecy. Joel Rosenberg, the author of a series of political thrillers and the book entitled *Epicenter: Why the Current Rumblings in the Middle East Will Change Your Future*, conjectures that current events are aligning in an eerie way with the Bible. His major premise is taken from a prophecy in Ezekiel 38-39 where he says Scripture indicates that in the last days, a confederation of Islamic states (including Iran, Sudan, Ethiopia, Turkey, Syria and Jordan among others) led by Russia will come against Israel in an all-out battle of staggering proportions. According to this interpretation of Ezekiel, the rest of the world will sit this one out and God Himself will intervene, showing the world His power by destroying the enemies of Israel and saving His people. Some biblical scholars believe that with a battle of this magnitude and the near-complete annihilation of the armed forces coming against Israel, the perfect scenario will be set for the Temple to be rebuilt as prophesied in Ezekiel 40. (Rosenberg, 2006)

When looking at current global events, it has become easier to imagine this possibility playing out. News broadcasts and newspaper headlines are filled with reports of Iran's pursuit of nuclear power, denial of the Holocaust and Iranian president Mahmoud Ahmadinejad's personal belief that he has been chosen by Allah to push the world towards a crisis so that the 12th Imam, the Islamic Messiah, will appear. There are accounts of Russia's uncharacteristically warm overtures to the Arab world while relations with the US continue to spiral downward. In Israel there is the unexpected news of the reestablishment of the ancient religious body, the Sanhedrin as well as the reappearance of the Red Heifer. When it comes to the fulfillment of prophecy, Bible scholars stress that the Bible has a track record of being incredibly literal and reliable. Considering the following headlines that have appeared over the last few years:

- "Members of reestablished Sanhedrin ascend Temple Mount" (Arutz Sheva December 8, 2004)
- "Partners in trade, Turkey and Russia eye closer defense cooperation" (Turkish Daily News, December 8, 2004)
- "Russians to sell missiles to Syria" (London Telegraph, February 17, 2005)
- "Wipe Israel 'Off the Map' says Iranian" (New York Times, October 27, 2005)
- "Sons of Aaron – the priestly tribe – convene in Jerusalem" (Arutz 7 July 7, 2007)

- "West Papua delegation donates gold for Holy Temple" (Arutz 7 October 8, 2007)
- "Ahmadinejad: 'American empire' nearing its end" (CNN – September 24, 2008)
- "Temple Institute has spent 27 million on preparation for rebuilding Jewish Temple" (The Age- November 14, 2009)
- "Turkey to increase trade with Iran despite sanctions" (Jerusalem Post, September 16, 2010)
- "Israel plays war game assuming Iran has nuclear bomb" (Reuters, May 17, 2010)
- Ahmadinejad called for the hastening of the Imam Al-Mahdi in his recent UN speech (September 23, 2010 http://www.scribd.com/doc/38037667/Mahmoud-Ahmadinejad-United-Nations-General-Assembly-FULL-Transcript)

The Interview

I approached the Jerusalem offices of the Temple Institute early on a Sunday morning with great anticipation and more than a little curiosity. With a history of misunderstandings and some negative press in the media, it is understandable that the Temple Institute employees are a little guarded. But after a thorough pre-interview session directed towards me by my host, Mr. Yitzchak Rueven, we settled into the business at hand. Mr. Rueven is a former harp maker and longtime friend of the Institute's director, Rabbi Chaim

Richman. He currently serves as the assistant director of the International Department of the Institute and he is as passionate as he is likable. It did not take long for us to fall into a fascinating discussion:

If the Jewish Temple was the place of God's presence, as your website indicates, where has God's presence been all these years since the Second Temple was destroyed in 70 AD?

"Good question. Hmm, how can I explain this? Obviously, God is everywhere and especially any place where we create an atmosphere for Him. The rebuilt Temple would be such a place. According to Exodus 25:8, God wanted the tabernacle built so that He would dwell "among" them; not necessarily "in" the tabernacle."

What is the significance of the Red Heifer?

"According to Numbers 19, the Red Heifer is needed in order to purify the priests and the people in order for Temple worship to resume. The heifer must be completely red. If it has more than two white hairs, it is disqualified."

Are you attempting to genetically engineer a Red Heifer and if so, how does that mesh with God's sovereignty?

"We are working with ranchers in Israel and in the US. Any sort of breeding is a form of genetic engineering, so we don't feel that we're taking matters into our own hands."

Do you currently have a Red Heifer?

"According to the Mishna, up until the destruction of the Second Temple, there have been only nine Red Heifers used to meet the purification needs of the people of Israel. According to ancient Jewish tradition, the tenth Red Heifer is associated with the Messianic era - the coming of the Messiah Himself. There has not been a Red Heifer born in Israel in nearly 2000 years. Perhaps God knew that it was not yet time. But in 2002, a Red Heifer was again born in Israel. Unfortunately, it was eventually disqualified because it grew three white hairs. As of the moment, I'm not aware of any others, but I am not always in the loop. We have had possibilities recently, but they were disqualified. When we find one that looks like a possibility, we separate it from the rest of the herd and watch it carefully. We try to keep it secret so that we don't set up the conditions for people to make pilgrimages to see it."

So, when you do actually get a Red Heifer, you will reinstitute animal sacrifice?

"Yes, but the altar has not, in fact, been prepared. However, the building of the altar would not itself be an impediment to the renewal of offerings. The location of the altar would be outside the Dome of the Rock. I would just like to add that we do not expect nor advocate an arrangement by which the Dome of the Rock would coexist with the altar. The Temple Mount is intended exclusively for the Holy Temple.

I know that people look at animal sacrifice as 'old school', but the way that it is performed is more humane than what happens in many commercial slaughter houses and there is no waste when it comes to the animal. We use all of it.

Recently, the Sanhedrin has reconvened. They are planning a Pascal Offering for this Passover." (Note: An April 7th, 2007 article in the online publication *Arutz 7* indicates that the Supreme Court in Israel has rejected the request to offer sacrifices on the Temple Mount.)

Recent archaeological discoveries have suggested that the original location of the Temple was south of the Dome of the

Rock and could actually be built without destroying the Islamic structure. What is your view on that?

"There is some disagreement with the position that the Temple can be rebuilt without destroying the Dome of the Rock. That information comes from one archaeologist and is based upon finding one cistern. It would certainly be convenient if that were true. But really, it doesn't make that much difference. It's not like the Muslims would be comfortable with any building on the Temple Mount.

Two thousand years of oral tradition indicates that the Holy of Holies is under the Dome of the Rock. To this day, Jews are forbidden to walk in certain places on the Temple Mount to avoid stepping into sacred places where only purified priests are allowed to go. This is where the Temple was located."

Some people believe that the centerpiece for the Holy of Holies, the Ark of the Covenant, was destroyed by the Babylonians. Others believe it's in the city of Axum, Ethiopia in the church of St. Mary of Zion, being protected by Ethiopian Monks. What do you believe about the location of the Ark of the Covenant?

"According to oral Jewish tradition, the Ark of the Covenant was buried under the Temple Mount. Solomon had a vision that the Temple would one day be destroyed and he made provisions for the Ark to be hidden prior to the Temple's destruction by the Babylonians. Twenty years ago an archaeological team went under the Temple Mount with Rabbi Getz and was within twenty yards of rediscovering the Ark.

Today, the Muslims are feverishly expanding the Temple Mount and in the process destroying Jewish artifacts while the Israeli government acquiesces. Access to the Temple Mount is becoming more and more difficult for Jews and other non-Muslims."

Some biblical scholars believe that the book of Ezekiel includes a prophecy that the end times will be punctuated by a confederation of Arab countries, led by Russia, coming against Israel in the battle of Gog and Magog. According to the prophecy, it seems that God will defend Israel and defeat the Russian and Arab armies and then Israel will be able to rebuild the temple. Looking at current events and the growing relationship between Russia and the Islamic world, can you foresee this biblical prophecy being fulfilled in the near future?

"Of course I see the possibility of that scenario playing out. I can see things moving in that direction, but we as Jews cannot just sit around and wait for this miracle to happen.

Our focus needs to be on preparation. And that's what the Temple Institute's main goal is: to educate and to prepare.

In addition, we must begin to conduct ourselves as a Jewish nation based on Jewish morality and justice. We need to get our act together as a nation. We can't second guess global events; we need to simply focus on doing what is right."

Your website indicates that redemption for the Jews as well as the world will come through the rebuilding of the Temple. Are you expecting the Messiah?

"The Temple is a conduit to heaven. It's a place for God's presence to be among us and a place for the Jewish people to gather together. Of course we are expecting the Messiah. But we must be prepared in advance for His coming."

Personal Responsibility

Mr. Rueven is a smart man and he understands the culture in which he lives. He knows that the goals of the Temple Institute are not necessarily the goals of the average Jewish citizen. But he believes that in order for Israel to be prepared for her future and the coming of the Messiah, people must be educated and they must take personal responsibility to be obedient to Jewish Scripture. People must be prepared to ask questions and be ready to answer questions. If nothing else, the current blend of international events and hints of biblical prophecy should remind people that we are moving towards something and we should live in light of that knowledge.

On my way back to the airport in Tel Aviv the afternoon following the interview, I thought back to the first day I arrived in Israel, the day the airport was closed, and I wondered about the fate of the man attempting to commit suicide. As I headed down the highway towards the airport, I looked over at my taxi driver and I asked him if he spent a lot of time going back and forth to the airport. He confirmed that he did, so I asked him if he had heard about the fate of the young man who had attempted to end his life at the airport a few days ago. He looked at me and slowly answered, "I don't know what happened."

"You mean you didn't hear anything about it?" I inquired.

He sighed, hesitated and said, "In Israel, sometimes it's better not to know."

"Well, then I'll ask someone at the airport. I'm sure that someone there will know," I countered.

"In Israel," he advised, "It's sometimes better not to know. But it's always better not to ask."

Yitzchak Rueven would disagree. He would probably say that if you are going to be obedient to God and be prepared for His future, it is always better to ask. And it is always better to know.

Sources:

1. Byers, Gary. "*Where Has the Lost Ark of the Covenant Been?*" Retrieved April 3, 2007 from http://www.christiananswers.net/q-abr/abr-a002.html
2. Gold, Dore. (2007) *The Fight for Jerusalem: Radical Islam, the West, and the Future of the Holy City.* Washington, D.C.: Regnery Publishing, Inc.
3. Reiter, Yitzchak (2005) *From Jerusalem to Mecca and Back: The Islamic Consolidation of Jerusalem.* Jerusalem: The Jerusalem Institute for Israel Studies.
4. Rosenberg, Joel. (2006) *Epicenter: Why the Current Rublings in the Middle East will Change Your Future*. Carol Stream, IL: Tyndale House Publishers, Inc.
5. "Temple Mount Travesty," *The Jerusalem Post,* July 14, 2007.

Is the Ark in Ethiopia?

A First-Person Interview with the High Priest of St. Mary of Zion church in Axum

Phil Johnson, Ph.D.
From Axum, Ethiopia
April 2007

Today, according to the Ethiopian Orthodox Church, the true Ark of the Covenant is housed in the Chapel of the Ark, a building adjacent to St. Mary of Zion Church in Axum, Ethiopia. The legend of the Ark says Menelek I, the son of King Solomon and the Queen of Sheba, brought the Ark from Jerusalem to Axum in the 900's BC right under the nose of the Temple priests and his father. According to several priests that I spoke to, the Ark has resided in Axum ever since.

Indeed, the whole culture of that city revolves around the Ark. When asking the people of that town about the Ark, they all report their fervent belief in the Ark and that God has given them the sacred duty of protecting it. They do not care who believes them. They do not care what others think. The townsfolk claim that the Ark is a source of great power and the source of God's power. One of the grand historical claims of Axum involves the stele field not far from the Chapel of the Ark. These solid granite obelisks represent the ancient rulers of the great Axumite Empire. According to the townspeople, it was the power of the Ark that erected these stone structures, some weighing more than 100 tons.

When I visited the Chapel of the Ark, I was told that no one is allowed inside save the Keeper of the Ark. According to a deacon of St. Mary of Zion, one man is chosen to guard the Ark. It is his sacred duty for his entire life. With his dying breath, he chooses his successor. The current Keeper of the Ark is a man named Aba Techlamariam. He is somewhere near seventy years old at this point. When I asked again if anyone else is *ever* allowed to see the Ark, I was told emphatically "no." According to the deacon, three years ago a Hungarian tourist attempted to rush the Chapel of the Ark to break through to see the Ark. Before he got anywhere close, 30 trained guards pounced on him. He was immediately arrested, taken back to Addis Ababa and deported back to his country. My guess is that he is not welcome to return.

My final interview of my brief trip to Axum was with the High Priest of the church of St. Mary of Zion himself. He had just finished a service and was tired, but he granted me a few minutes. He gave me a summary of what I had already heard from my guide, the High Priest of St. Pentala and a church deacon. But my final question was this: “Sir, are you aware of the prophecies of Ezekiel 38-39 as well as what’s currently going on in the Middle East? If so, and if this prophetic scenario plays out making the building of the Third Temple possible, will you return the Ark to the Temple and allow it to sit in the Holy of Holies where it originally rested?” His answer was not burdened by thought or hesitation. “Never,” he said. “Never will we return the Ark. It is ours, given to us by God and it is not a gift to be returned or given away. We will keep it until the end of time, until the end of the world as we know it. We will keep it until this world burns with fire.” Question asked; question answered.

Sources:

1. Hancock, Graham. (1992) *The Sign and the Seal: The Quest for the Lost Ark of the Covenan*t. New York: Crown Books.
2. McCall, Thomas. *Where is the Ark of the Covenant?* Retrieved May 5, 2007 from http://www.levitt.com/essays/ark.html

An Interview with Hamas

Phil Johnson, Ph.D.
From Damascus, Syria
October 2009

In October of 2009, I had the opportunity to sit down with Talal Nasser, a senior Hamas official in their office in Damascus, Syria. Hamas is designated by the West as a terrorist organization and is viewed as a resistance movement in the Arab world. The most recent and significant clash with Israel occurred in the winter of 2008-2009 and was called Operation Cast Lead by the Israelis and was known as the Gaza Massacre to the Muslim world. The following is an interview that attempts to shed light on the purposes, philosophy and goals of Hamas as a political and military organization.

What is your role in Hamas?

I am one of the members in Hamas. I am responsible for PR

and just recently I gained a new position in the political decisions making area of Hamas. I am currently wanted by the Israeli forces because I am one of the founders of the al-Qassam Brigade – the military wing of Hamas.

Is your life in danger from the Israelis?

I have security, but I am not afraid. Why? Because we have a superior target – or goal which is to kick the occupiers out from the land. We work for our people and for our interests.

What is the strength of Hamas after the latest war with Israel that ended in January 2009?

The movement is strong and was strong even before the Israeli Holocaust in Gaza. Our popularity is growing – as a movement because of the martyrs who gave their lives for this cause.

Hamas showed a good example for a resistance movement – in how they handled everything from their vision to distributing food to those in need during the war. According to a Swedish NGO, Hamas's popularity is now at 82.2% within the Palestinian West Bank.

How many people were killed in Gaza, including civilians?

We consider all people killed in this war as being from Hamas – children, women and men. But as the real fighters go, 89 fighters were killed. This does not include the number of policemen and civilians.

Do you believe that you have impacted Israel's position in what you consider to be occupied territory? Has significant pain and destruction been inflicted upon Israel?

Israel is a criminal state and they never respect any international laws. If we don't make any pain against them, they won't accept a cease-fire. An Israeli writer said that what Hamas's army did, no other Arab army could do or has done. And the Israelis were afraid that Hamas could launch rockets against Tel Aviv. And they were afraid that we could kidnap more soldiers – and we could and we did, but the Israelis bombed our position and killed their own soldiers.

So what we did in the Gaza war was create the situation where even our enemies would have to respect us.

My contacts in Israeli indicate that rockets from Gaza are still being fired into Israel on a daily basis, even after the ceasefire on January 18th

Hamas hasn't launched any rockets since the ceasefire – and Israel lies. Well, actually, Hamas launched about 20 rockets after the ceasefire to show that while Israel started the war, Hamas finished it. But now we don't launch any rockets not because we are afraid of Israel, but because we wanted to limit the suffering of our people.

My sources inside Gaza say that there are gangs that have risen up and that are challenging the power of Hamas. What is your response to that?

There is no mafia and no gangs – but there are other Palestinian groups that don't believe as Hamas believes. There were gangs, but Hamas has finished them off.

You are quoted in the Israeli publication *Haaretz* as encouraging Palestinians to rise up against the Palestinian Authority and President Mahmoud Abbas. What is the purpose of this challenge?

Abbas has now become a symbol of a liar and a traitor to the Palestinian people in the whole Muslim world. For example, Abbas said that we have no prisoners of conscience in the West Bank and then after two or three days, he said we're going to release all of those political prisoners.

Abbas also tried to make it sound like the Hamas leaders ran away during the war. But they didn't. Abbas is not acting like a president of the Palestinian people. He is a mouthpiece of the Fatah movement. He is definitely a traitor. I have received many messages on my mobile phone begging me to not put my hand with the dirty hand of Abbas.

Could Hamas become the legitimate political party of all Palestinians, including the West Bank?

Abbas stays in power only because of the support of the Israelis. Netanyahu said, a couple of days ago, he has two missions: Keep the settlements in the West Bank and protect the Palestinian Authority and Abbas. Even the head of police from Ramallah was in a private meeting here in Damascus and he said that Hamas could take over the West Bank in just a few hours.

Are there any Hamas training camps in Syria?

We are in Syria and in other countries as a media office – to represent the cause. And we want to increase the awareness of the culture of resistance. And the Israeli's are liars and are always saying that we have these things, these training camps, but we don't.

What about weapon smuggling?

We are more than happy to get any weapons from any states – even from the USA who supports Israel. We don't care what others say – we're concerned with how to get weapons to protect our people. And we even buy weapons from the Israeli mafia who sell them to us to buy heroin. Our main mission is to protect our people and to get weapons from anywhere. And of course they are smuggled through Syria.

Describe the relationships Hamas has with Iran.

We have a good relationship – warm relations with Iran as

we bond over the culture of resistance. And the US, every day creates a story to attack an Arab or an Arab country, so it's not new to us.

We look to the US as the source of terrorism; therefore, we have to unify to fight this terrorism. The US occupies Iraq and they've killed more than 1.5 million Iraqis. And today, the American people believe that Rumsfeld was a big liar.

If they (the Americans) talk about Democracy in Iraq, why don't they accept democracy in the Palestinian territories when Hamas won the election? So we have to unify our efforts with nations like Iran to combat the US and Israeli terrorism.

What are your predictions and thoughts about Iran's Nuclear weapons?

Israel has more than 250 nuclear heads. And the US has nuclear weapons that can destroy the world 4 times over. Same as Russia. Why do they allow these countries to have these weapons and then forbid Muslims to have these weapons? The US is the first and only nation to use these weapons and they used them on Japan.

Iran has the right to obtain nuclear weapons. They will use them against others who try to occupy Iranian land or others who attempt to use nuclear weapons against them.

If Iran achieves nuclear weapons, will President Ahmadinejad make good on this threat to wipe Israel off the face of the map?

No, we will take care of that ourselves. We will knock off Israel and we'll be happy to get help from any country – Syria, Sudan, anyone. We will never look at our suffering as some people look at it. Israel has used weapons, chemical weapons and no one in the world talks about that. So we will work hard to knock Israel off the map.

So is that your ultimate goal, to destroy Israel?

Our main goal is to occupy all of Palestine and to push Israel to the sea or back to their countries. We are over 10 million refugees, but we will return home soon.

I will believe that Israel will soon witness an uprising from within that will weaken them. And I believe that there is a high rate of emigration. People are leaving Israel. All of those immigrants who came to Israel were looking for security and money – today they have neither.

If you go to the streets here in the Damascus refugee camp and you ask the Palestinian children where they are from, they will tell you they are from Ramallah or Haifa, even though they were born in Syria. If you ask Israeli children where they are from, they will always say, Russia, Ukraine, Poland, etc. even though they were born in Israel. Let them go back.

Europe has a large Muslim population. Will Europe experience a backlash of violence from Muslim communities because of their support of Israel?

The Europeans are supporting the Zionists and because of this they will feel the brunt of the Islamic uprising in Europe. Europe talks about human rights and freedom and yet they support Israel when Israel initiated a siege on Gaza's 1.5 million people.

When Hamas and the Palestinians capture an Israeli soldier from his tank, all European nations send delegates to Damascus to seek the release of the prisoner. Meanwhile, we have 12,000 Palestinian prisoners, but no one talks about it.

What's your prediction regarding Europe over the next year or two? Will there be Muslim uprisings there?

We know that there are Arabs living in Europe. They see how the Europeans support Israel, but we cannot evaluate their ultimate reactions just yet.

It's the same in the US – there are many Arab Muslims living there. And we know that the Israelis use many US-made weapons against Gaza- and so far nothing's happened in the US regarding an uprising. But it's like a volcano and at any moment it can explode.

(Authors note: Since this interview, a European court ruled that crucifixes are no longer allowed in Italian classrooms. This was partially motivated by the Muslim population. In addition, Switzerland just voted to ban the building of Islamic Minarets in their countries. This indicates that tensions are increasing in Europe regarding their relationship with their Muslim minorities.)

What is Hamas's Relationship with the Russian Government?

We started a political relationship after the election of Hamas to power. We have mutual interests. We have political ties with Russia. And we are ready to have ties with any nation that recognizes our rights and just like Israel has the support of the US. Russia helps us in the region. We have ties with them because they see our rights.

Does Russia support you with money and weapons?

No.

Does Hamas have any influence on US college campuses?

We don't have ties with anyone on the campuses. We have some ties with former President Carter. And sometimes some American human rights groups come to Syria to discuss the condition of the Palestinian peoples.

Is there any funding from the US coming to Hamas from any source at all?

We don't have donations from the US or Europe as we are designated a terror group. But if terrorism means that we adhere to our religion and adhere to our resistance, then we are ready to say that we are a terrorist group.

Do you have any final predictions for Hamas over the next five years?

We will have our state and we will have our land. We have the will for the fight, but Israel does not. Israeli soldiers will bomb us, but they won't fight. Hamas soldiers are fighters. When Hamas fighters go off to war, their mothers say goodbye. When Israeli sons go off to war, their mothers cry.

Living Out of the Shadow of Bin Laden

Osama bin Laden's former bodyguard opens up

Phil Johnson, Ph.D.
From Sana'a, Yemen
June 2010

Located on the Arabian Peninsula in Southwest Asia, Yemen is a beautiful, mysterious and timeless country, filled with amazingly warm and friendly people. But Western governments have currently rated Yemen as too dangerous to visit unless you have "essential" business there. Though I've never been one to put much stock in such ratings, I will concede that Yemen is the poorest and most tribal nation on the Arabian Peninsula. It is also home to the terrorist organization known as al-Qaeda Arabian Peninsula (AQAP) – a franchise of the regular al-Qaeda.

Yemen is on the brink of becoming a second Afghanistan where al-Qaeda will find it easy to recruit disaffected youth given the high poverty rate and diminishing oil supplies.

Similar to Pakistan and Afghanistan, Yemen has plenty of weapons and men experienced in guerrilla warfare who resent U.S. policies and have tribal and inspirational ties to al-Qaeda. In this environment it is very difficult to discourage contact between impressionable young men and their jihadist heroes. If anti-American sentiment continues to grow, you can expect more trouble from this region. *

So, it was in this context that I sat down with Mr. Nasser al-Bahri, the former bodyguard of al-Qaeda leader, Osama bin Laden. According to Michael Campbell (2010) of the *London Times,* al-Bahri's new book entitled *In the Shadow of bin Laden* is the first to emerge from bin Laden's inner circle. Al-Bahri is also viewed as a wealth of intelligence information for the CIA because of his close direct relationship with bin Laden. For me, Nasser Al-Bahri, whose nickname was "The Killer," was warm, charming and hospitable as we sat in his apartment with my translator, Ameen Abdullah and two of al-Bahri's associates.

Tell me about your new book. It's called "*In the Shadow of bin Laden,"* and was just released in April, correct?
Yes, it was published in Paris and it is about me, about my life and my journey through jihad and back again. But I'm not at liberty to speak much about it now. **

I heard that France wouldn't grant you a visa so you could visit and promote the book?

I didn't apply for a visa – I learned that I was refused a visa from the media. I heard that I asked for the visa from the embassy from France – but I never asked for a visa. The publisher wanted me to come to France, but I said I wouldn't come unless there could be an official invitation between the French government and the Yemeni government.

Tell me about your days in Afghanistan.

I didn't begin in Afghanistan. I first went to Bosnia. It wasn't about terrorism – it was about going for a religious purpose...to help those who were Muslim victims of what was going on in Bosnia. First I went to Bosnia, then Somalia, then Tajikistan then Afghanistan. I began at the age of 22.

The main purpose of this type of jihad was to go and help the poor people and to give them food and to provide services. Yes, I had a weapon, but it was just to protect myself from anyone who might want to harm me or kill me. I went to help. The media talks about bad things and change the truth about jihad and the reality of jihad. The media says that the mujahideen only fought the Serbs, and doesn't mention the humanitarian efforts of the mujahideen.

After Bosnia, I went to Somalia, then on to Tajikistan and then back to Afghanistan. This is when I met Osama bin Laden.

Tell me about your time with bin-Laden.

As I said, I was returning from Tajikistan to Yemen, and was going through Afghanistan – I stayed for nine months and I met bin Laden and was trained by him, along with other young men for al-Qaeda. I joined al-Qaeda and eventually I became bin Laden's personal bodyguard.

What were your responsibilities as his bodyguard?

I did a lot of things – first and foremost I was bin Laden's bodyguard – to protect him and keep him safe. Sometimes I played a principle role representing al-Qaeda towards new recruits. I also trained the new guys who joined al-Qaeda for jihad – the military type of jihad - between the years 1996-2000.

When was the last time you saw bin-Laden?

In Kandahar, Afghanistan before the event of the USS Cole attack. Two months before this event.

Did you know about the USS Cole attack in advance?

No.

Did you know about the 9/11 attacks in advance?

In general, everyone knew about the fighting between al-Qaeda and America. But I didn't know how, what or where the next attack would come from? But I did know something was going to happen? Sometimes, when we saw different guys disappear or families move, it indicated that al-Qaeda was up to something; that something was coming.

When 9/11 happened, what was your response?

When 9/11 happened, I was in jail – in prison. I had returned to Yemen in 2000 and that's when the USS Cole incident happened. I heard that the government was looking for all al-Qaeda members and I tried to escape to Afghanistan, but the police caught me at the airport trying to leave.

When 9/11 happened, The FBI came to me in prison and the officer showed me the newspaper and pictures and I knew about this event through the FBI when they investigated me.

Why were you arrested if your version of jihad was just about helping others?

I didn't do anything criminal in Yemen, only outside of Yemen. The law in Yemen says that it's OK to be a mujahideen. But the government arrested me after USS Cole bombing. I didn't have anything to do with this bombing, but the government arrested me to protect itself.

Was the Yemeni government under significant pressure from the US to arrest people in connection to the USS Cole?

In the beginning there was no pressure. But after the problem and activities of al-Qaeda in Yemen, it put the government in a situation where they had to do something – take some action. I was part of that action.

When you were working for bin Laden, what was he like? What was his character like?

He had a very strong, very determined character... he was determined to destroy the West. The truth is that Osama bin-Laden's main goal was to fight America – he says this all the time – it's not a secret.

And do you feel the same way?

At the beginning I was with him – I completely agreed with him. After the 9/11attack on civilian people, I stopped agreeing. But the American people should know their government and they have the power to change their government if they don't like it or don't agree with it.

When the FBI showed you the photos of 9/11 and you saw how many people died, what did you think? Did you think this was a great victory for bin Laden and for al-Qaeda? Or did you think that this was a terrible loss of human life?

You must understand my way of thinking. In my opinion, I know America has killed a lot of people in Iraq, Somalia and Arab countries. I know that they help and support Israel. But we don't need to attack civilian people inside America. A lot of people in al-Qaeda agree with me on this. For example, Mustafa Abu Yazid – a top leader in al-Qaeda thinks the same as me on this. ***

A lot of people in al-Qaeda, they refuse to kill civilian people inside America. Yes, we hate America, and we want to fight them, but it doesn't give us the right to kill the civilians. I know that the government of the US is terroristic, but we don't have to be like them. Your government is a terrorist entity – they kill in Iraq and Somalia. Yes, America is a terrorist nation.

Where do you get most of your current information? What media outlets? What websites?

I get some information from local news, from the media, the Internet – Arab language sites - and some other sources. But the information from my other sources is private – secret. It is from individuals who provide information and I can't share it with you now. Maybe if I get to know you better in the future.

What is your view on Iran getting nuclear weapons?

Every country must be able to protect itself. They must have the appropriate weapons to defend themselves. Iran's Shiite history shows that they only fight other Muslims. Not the Jews, not the Christians. The Shiite Muslims only fight Christians or Jews when they feel that their business or interests are threatened.

Iran's leaders have stated publicly that they want to wipe Israel off the map. Do you agree with this statement?

I wish Israel would vanish from the map, but Iran will not vanish Israel from the map. Other global leaders have said the same thing, but didn't do anything. Other Arab leaders have said the same thing, but nothing happens.

But Israel knows who will vanish them from the maps – the REAL MUSLIMS. This came from a statement from the leader of Israel – who says that Israel will vanish because of the new generation of Muslims who truly follow the prophet Mohamed.

Give me your view of the recent Turkish flotilla situation between Israel and Turkey:

It's no longer Arab governments who are fighting against Israel. The local people - even in Israel - are now fighting Israel. It is a shift. Israel thinks only Muslim governments are fighting her. But from the Arab perspective, Israel is now being fought by average citizens - the people who have the Islamic idea.

Israel's view is that maybe the flotilla was smuggling guns and weapons – Israel has problems with Hamas – Israel must first realize that they don't have reasons to fight the boat from Turkey – but they should have gone inside the boat and inspected it. All the people on board had diplomatic passports – they were not members of al-Qaeda or Hamas. They are humanitarian people. They were attacked first and were only trying to defend themselves.

Some non-political intelligence assessments I received contend that this was a brilliant plan by Turkey to draw Israel out into international waters, bate them and create an explosive situation to further damage Israel's global reputation.

I believe that those on the flotilla were innocent humanitarians – the media creates lies. In addition, when the media shows the pictures and Westerners see the beards on some of the humanitarians, they assume they are terrorist – because of the beards.

I'll give you an example, the opinion in Yemen is that anyone with an American passport is Jewish – because of the US support of Israel. Obviously that is not true – it's a stereotype. In the same way, people in the West think that any man with a beard is a terrorist.

And don't forget, when the boat was boarded, it was still in international waters.

Currently, 90% of Israelis believe that the US administration is not supportive of their country. (Rosenberg, 2010) What is your opinion about US president, Barak Obama and do you believe that the current US administration is still supporting Israel?

This business of not supporting Israel is not true- it's just politics. America still supports Israel. Hillary Clinton is Jewish. The Minister of Defense is Jewish. The head of national security is Jewish. They all support Israel.

When Obama was in the election process, he visited Israel and gave his word of support for Israel. He told Israel that they needed to wait while he made a good picture between America and Arab nations.

There has been ongoing conflict between US and Iran, Iraq, Palestine and the many other Arab nations. Now the people in these nations are against the US, so now America wants to make a good picture, but the problem is that Israel is making trouble for the US, because of their actions.

And look at Europe. If a particular government hates Muslims - like in France where they say that the women can't wear the hijabs (veils) then we will hate them. Plus, this allows good recruitment propaganda for al-Qaeda for new members. There is freedom for every religion in Europe except for Muslims.

But does Yemen provide freedom of religion? Does Yemen allow churches?

There are no churches in Yemen, but they government protects the Yemeni Jews. There is a statement from Mohammed that says that there can be only one religion in Arab land. Do you see a mosque in the Vatican? Do you see a synagogue there? Why should there be churches or synagogues on Arab land?

As we close, give me your predications for the next 5 years for the global community.

- Will Israel still exist five years from now?
  I think that in the next five years, there will be a big separation between Israel and the Arab people – more than ever before. Israel has tried in the past to make a good impression with Arabs but because of all the current Israeli aggression, the relationship will deteriorate.

- Will Iran get and use nuclear weapons?
  They will get it. They won't use it. America thinks that Iran is like Saddam Hussein when he was in Iraq. The US just uses it as card against Iran. Even if Iran got this weapon, they won't use it. They just want to be equal to other nations and balance the power.

- Will the Palestinians get their own state?
  I don't think so.

- Will Osama bin Laden be captured in the next five years?
  I hope that America can never catch him, but if they catch him, then that's his destiny from God.

- Do you know where bin Laden is?

  Of course many journalists have asked me this question. The answer is: I don't know anything. But if I knew, I would never say. Even though al-Qaeda has now tried to assassinate me several times because I am no longer a member, I would never say where bin Laden is – if I knew. I still miss the early jihad days and helping other Muslims in war torn, oppressed countries.

Special Notes:

*Links have already been made between Yemen and Umar Farouk Abdulmutallab, the Nigerian accused of trying to blow up a Detroit-bound flight from Amsterdam on Christmas Day and also Major Midal Malik Hasan, the Army psychiatrist accused of killing 13 people in November at Fort Hood, Texas.

**According to reviews, in addition to al-Bahri's personal life, the book also includes information about bin Laden's prowess on the volleyball court as well as on the soccer field – but he never takes off his turban! It also talks about bin Laden's passion for racehorses, jealousies between some of his wives and how he won't give his children any of his fortune – it's all earmarked for Islam. (Times of London, April 18, 2010)

***Yazid was killed in Afghanistan/Pakistan border by a Predator strike just a few days before this interview. According to Bill Roggio, (2010) "Yazid is one of al Qaeda's most important leaders, and he will be difficult to replace. He served as al Qaeda's leader in Afghanistan and in what the terror group refers to as the Khorasan, a region that encompasses large areas of Afghanistan, Pakistan, Uzbekistan, Tajikistan, and Iran. The Khorasan is considered by jihadists to be the place where they will inflict the first defeat against their enemies in the Muslim version of Armageddon. The final battle is to take place in the Levant - Israel, Syria, and Lebanon."

According to Thomas Joscelyn, (2010) of the *Weekly Standard,* the West has misunderstood the nature of the 9/11 dissent within the ranks of al-Qaeda and the Taliban. The disagreement wasn't about harming innocent people in the US. Yazid's objection to the 9/11 attacks was a tactical objection. The concern was that the attacks would wake the "sleeping giant" of the US and that the result would be a devastating counterattack.

Sources –

Campbell, Michael. (2010) "Bin Laden, a secret fan of footie and Monty." Times Online, April 19, 2010.

http://www.timesonline.co.uk/tol/news/world/afghanistan/article7100865.ece#cid=OTC-RSS&attr=797093

Joscelyn, Thomas. (2010) "On the Death of Mustafa Abu Yazid: The top terrorist's career dispels some myths about our enemies." The Weekly Standard, June 1, 2010. http://www.weeklystandard.com/blogs/death-mustafa-abu-yazid

Roggio, Bill, (2010) "Top al Qaeda leader Mustafa Abu Yazid confirmed killed in airstrike in North Waziristan" The Long War Journal, May 31, 2010. http://www.longwarjournal.org/archives/2010/05/top_al_qaeda_leader_1.php

Rosenberg, Joel (2010) "Fewer than 1-in-10 Israelis believe President Obama is pro-Israel because of the administration's long string of deeply unfriendly statements and actions." Charisma Magazine Online, July 8, 2010. http://www.charismamag.com/index.php/in-the-news/28876-on-defense-obama-tries-to-improve-us-israeli-relations

Military Coup or Street Elections?

Egypt's Crisis 2013

Phil Johnson, Ph.D.
From Cairo, Egypt
July 6, 2013

One year after Egypt's first free democratic elections, President Mohamed Morsi has been forced to step down. Depending on who you talk with, the president's ouster was the result of a military coup or it was the decision of the masses who decided that they didn't like the direction of their country and took to the streets for a "snap election" of sorts. Here's a concise update on the situation:

June 30:

Massive demonstrations across Egypt (the largest protests in Egypt's history) called for President Morsi to step down. Reasons for public dissatisfaction included the free-falling economy, frequent power outages, Morsi's abuse of power, the crafting of an
Islamist-leaning constitution, lack of protection for the rights of women and minorities and failure to create an inclusive government.

July 3rd:

The Egyptian military announced that Morsi's presidency was over and that the constitution would be suspended.

July 4th:

The military appointed Chief Justice of the constitutional court, Adli Mansour, as interim president. The military stated that new presidential elections would be held and a new constitution created.

July 5th:

A coalition of conservative groups, led by the Muslim Brotherhood, have promised to protect the legitimacy of Morsi's presidency - the result has been increased violence.

On Friday, July 5th, more than 30 were killed in clashes between supporters and opposition groups. More than 1000 were wounded. (Al Jezeera English)

July 6th:

Gunmen killed a Coptic Christian priest in the increasingly difficult to control Sinai peninsula. According to security sources, he was dragged from his car and riddled with bullets. This could be the first sectarian attack since Morsi was forced from office. Coptic Pope Tawadros, leader of Egypt's Christian minority, has come under fire for his support of the removal of Morsi.

Those who support Morsi's presidency state that Morsi was democratically elected and that he is the legitimate leader of Egypt. The people made their choice and if they want a new choice, then they need to wait three more years for a new presidential election. Therefore, the action of the army to take over is viewed as a military coup in direct opposition to the principles of democracy. Supporters also site the unwillingness of the opposition to accept key positions in the government and to participate in the democratic process. Morsi stated in a speech on July 2nd, that he would defend his presidency with his life, if necessary. He is now under house arrest.

The Egyptian opposition to Morsi's presidency (The Tamarod movement, among others) views the action of the military to remove Morsi as a response to the will of the people - NOT a coup. After all, it's hard to ignore the largest protest movement in Egypt's history - and according to some sources, the largest protest movement in the history of the world.

Those opposed to Morsi's rule say that they and the military are one- and that the military is acting on behalf of the best interest of Egypt. In the midst of this new chapter in Egyptian self-determination, there is also a visible rise in anti-Obama and anti-American sentiment. Many of those who opposed Morsi's presidency and the influence of the Muslim Brotherhood accuse US President Obama of supporting the Brotherhood's regime and supporting terrorism. Arguments can be made that Obama is supporting democracy - in any form, but that argument doesn't hold water with those who feel that the US administration is siding with the Muslim Brotherhood and its agenda. The resounding cry is simply, "Leave Egypt alone and stop supporting terrorists." They are quick to remind the world that the Muslim Brotherhood is the parent organization of Hamas and al Qaeda and has produced the likes of Osama bin Laden and Ayman Zawahari. So, they ask, why exactly is Obama supporting this organization?

Al-Qaeda is now offering to rescue the Muslim Brotherhood movement in Egypt by sending in fighters. And according to *Al Jazeera English*, "A new Islamist group has also announced its formation in Egypt, calling the army's ousting of Morsi a declaration of war on its faith and threatening to use violence to impose Islamic law. Ansar al-Shariah in Egypt said it would gather arms and start training its members, in a statement posted on an online forum for fighters in the country's Sinai region on Friday."

In the end, Egyptians are continuing to take their fate into their own hands. While it's unlikely that Morsi will regain the presidency, the conflict is far from over. Will more blood be shed? Unfortunately, yes. Will some groups become more radicalized? Probably. But as of now, tens of millions of Egyptians decided, after a year of Morsi's rule, that they didn't want their country to go in the direction of the Brotherhood and Sharia law. Millions of thinking Muslims and Christians decided that they want to participate in a civilized, pluralistic society that allows for freedom of speech, thinking and religion - and that they will not become victims of radicalism in any form. Maybe that's the real story.

Benghazi: Unanswered Questions

The Diminishing Reality of Safety and Truth

Phil Johnson, Ph.D.
From Benghazi, Libya
April 20, 2013

If you ask a Libyan, he will tell you that Egypt is dangerous and out of control these days. If you ask an Egyptian, he will tell you to steer clear of Libya; it is filled with terrorists.

Different places; different perceptions. I've worked in both locations and at times each perception is correct. And at times each perception is wrong. But perception isn't truth. And the issue of truth is what keeps nagging at the heart of the Benghazi issue. It's been a little more than two years since the Libyan Revolution rid the world of Muammar Gaddafi. Libyans remain optimistic, if a bit more realistic that rebuilding a nation isn't the same as downloading a file from the Internet. It's going to take some time. They will also tell you that Libyans are peaceful and have no interest in terrorism. They will tell you that Libya is safe. At times that seems true. Until it isn't.

On September 11, 2012, Ambassador Chris Stevens and three other American nationals found out that their world wasn't safe. An armed group of militants attacked the diplomatic mission in Benghazi on the evening of the 11th. Their weapons included rocket-propelled grenades (RPGs), AK-47s, hand grenades, mortars and heavy machine guns. A second attack, which began just after midnight, occurred on the nearby CIA annex. (Murphy, Webb 2013). In the end, four Americans lay dead: Chris Stevens, Sean Smith, Ty Woods and Glen Doherty.

Seven months after their untimely deaths, questions remain: What did the US president and his senior staff know and when did they know it? Was it possible to send help to our citizens in Benghazi? If so, why didn't we? Who is responsible for these attacks? Was it a spontaneous escalation based on a protest regarding a YouTube video that insulted the Prophet, Mohammed? Or was it a preplanned, calculated assault on Western interests using heavy weapons? Why were previous requests for more security from the Benghazi mission left unfulfilled? After all, there had been several acts of violence prior to September 11th and Ambassador Steven's diary itself noted the increasing threat of extremism and the growing influence al Qaeda. (CNN, 2012.) And why have we not heard from the survivors of that attack? Where are the answers? Where is the truth? If something is being covered up, for what purpose?

Senator Lindsey Graham is calling for testimony from the survivors and he believes that they are being intimidated into silence. He recently stated this: "[The administration is] refusing to give us the id entity of the survivors and allow them to come to Congress to be interviewed. I've talked to a couple and their story is chilling. They're scared to death to come forward without some institutional support." (Foxnewsinsider.com. 2013.) White House press secretary, Jay Carney denies that anyone has been asked to remain silent. So, why aren't the survivors telling their story? On April 18, 2013, Speaker of the House, John Boehner, posted from his official website that the five House committees charged with investigating the attack in Benghazi will soon release a progress report. He says, "We are determined to get to the truth regarding the terrorist attack on our Mission in Benghazi, Libya, in which four Americans lost their lives." This thing is not over. But not much is any clearer.

Here in Benghazi, answers are no more forthcoming. I sat down with Mr. Fateh Younis Elkhashmi, the chief editor of the New Quryna, Libya's largest Arabic newspaper, to discuss the region and questions that continue to itch at the wound of Benghazi. When asked about the possibility that the US is engaging in secret wars in North Africa waged by US special forces or private security firms, Mr. Elkhashmi remains vague, but offers this statement: "Everyone knows that the US does whatever it wants. There are few nights that we don't hear US drones in the sky. We know that the US is looking for terrorist activity in Benghazi, in Derna and in the Green Mountains. We know they are here. We know what they are looking for." It sounds like blowback may have played some part in this incident.

Another speculation is that Ambassador Stevens was collecting weapons that were left over after the revolution. Some say that he was coordinating the transfer of heavy weapons from Libya to Turkey and then to Syria to aid in the support of the Syrian rebels - effectively dealing in an off-radar weapons trade program. Since those who are fighting against President Assad in Syria include jihadists, supplying them with heavy weapons would be a political problem for the US - if it is confirmed that we are indeed arming extremists.

According to Mr. Elkhashmi, since the revolution, weapons are in the hands of everyone. Are they being collected and sent to Syria? Maybe, he concedes, weapons are in the hands of those who are going from Libya to Syria to fight the jihad, but otherwise, he doesn't know for sure. What he does think is that if the US and its allies wanted President Assad gone from Syria, then he'd already be gone. But Elkhashmi believes that the US is uncertain of the regional outcome if Assad goes. Who would take over? And getting rid of Assad would likely destabilize the region in regards to Israel and Lebanon. Time will tell, but it doesn't look like Bashar Assad will go willingly. But neither did Mr. Gaddafi.

Not a whole lot is clear these days. The world is seemingly more complex with more shadows and less truth, even as the sheer amount of information available has increased exponentially. Aside from the big question of how the US failed to protect its representatives abroad, the question remains: Exactly who was behind the attacks. Within hours of the events of September 11th, Ansar al Sharia, the largest Islamist group in Libya, took responsibility for the attack. However, a week later, Ansar al Sharia leader, Mohammad al-Zahawi denied that the brigade had any role in the attack, but said the group would not give up its weapons. "We are in a battle with the liberals, the secularists and the remnants of Gadhafi," he told the BBC. (Maher, 2012.) The New Quryna's Elkhashmi affirms that Ansar al Sharia was not responsible for the attack. He says that Libyans - including members of Ansar al Sharia - simply want good lives and the freedom to follow their faith. But that begs one final, but very important question: What if the perception of "following your faith" requires you to remove obstacles - or your perception of obstacles - that stand in its way? According to an interview given to BBC news, (Maher, 2012) Ansar al Sharia leader, al-Zahawi, admitted to destroying and desecrating Sufi shrines in Benghazi because his group views them as idolatrous. "It is a religious duty to remove these shrines because people worship the deceased and this is prohibited. It's is not me who says so but rather our religion."

So what does a group with an extreme interpretation of the Koran and Sharia law do with the existence of a YouTube video that insults Islam? What do they do with societies that believe in, but do not always agree with, the free speech of others? What happens if a group, even a relatively small and loosely formed group like Ansar al Sharia, views "free speech" as a "shrine" that stands in the way of being able to follow what you believe is the one true religion. And what if you believe your interpretation of that religion is the correct one. What does your religious duty compel you to do? Does another person's free speech and personal freedom of conscience then stand in the way of another's faith? After all, everyone's in favor of free speech until they don't like what's being said. At what point do we curtail freedom of expression and at what point do we simply trust God to deal with those who insult Him or who choose not to follow Him in the way that you think they should?

When asked whether he believes that the attack on the Benghazi mission was the spontaneous result of a protest against a video or a preplanned attack, Elkhashmi gives a shrug and says, "Who knows?" If the most reliable news source in Libya knows the answer to this question, they're not saying. Former Secretary of State Hillary Clinton put it like this when answering this same question before Congress, "What difference at this point does it make?" I'm sure it makes a difference for the families and friends of those people who lost their lives. It makes a difference that governments seem incapable of telling the truth and serving the interests of their citizens. It makes a difference that some radical perceptions are

colliding with reality and the result is producing a more dangerous and unstable world. It makes a difference that the actions of a few extremists impact the image of a billion people.

All of this matters. But it's also important to remember that only a relatively small percentage of people are creating the chaos. Most people who have strong faith and religious values aren't interested in removing "shrines" and limiting free speech. Most are interested in the freedom to pursue their beliefs, influence those around them, pursue opportunities and respect those who disagree with them. As we found out recently during the Boston Marathon, it only takes a few people to create instability and insecurity in the world. The very unpredictable nature of danger makes it possible for a very few to disrupt the lives of many. With truth and safety becoming rare commodities, people are going to have to think hard about where to find truth, how to interpret truth, and where to place their feelings and longings for security. My guess is that the world is not going to become safer or more predictable.

Sources:

"CNN finds, returns journal belonging to late U.S. Ambassador" by the CNN Wire Staff: September 23, 2012

http://edition.cnn.com/2012/09/22/world/africa/libya-ambassador-journal

Maher, Ahmed. (September 18, 2012) *"Meeting Mohammad Ali al-Zahawi of Libyan Ansar al-Sharia"* http://www.bbc.co.uk/news/world-africa-19638582

Murphy, Jack and Brandon Webb (2013). Benghazi: The Definitive report. New York, NY: HarperCollins Inc. pp. 25–58. ISBN 9780062276919

"Sen. Lindsey Graham: Benghazi Survivors *"Scared to Death to Come Forward" After Obama Admin Told Them to Keep Quiet"* (April 17, 2013) http://foxnewsinsider.com/2013/03/17/sen-lindsey-graham-benghazi-survivors-scared-to-death-to-come-forward-after-obama-admin-told-them-to-keep-quiet/#ixzz2QvN 8z9Gch

Lebanon: Caught in Syria's War

Phil Johnson, Ph.D.
From Beirut, Lebanon
March 13, 2014

Lebanon is complicated. There's no other way to describe it. Walking down busy Hamra Street you will see miniskirts and hijabs side by side. Lebanon has 19 official religions. There's the Lebanese army and then there is Hezbollah. The Lebanese coalition government finally put its pieces in place, but new elections are "scheduled" for May, which gives this government an expiration date of about three months. Yes, it's a complicated place. But nothing is more complicated - or divisive - than the issue of the war in Syria.

Lebanon is deeply split over this issue which seems increasingly divided between the Shiite and Sunni sects of Islam. Here are some insights about what's going on:

The Ongoing War in Syria:

For the last three years, resistance forces have been trying to overthrow the Syrian regime, led by President Bashar Assad. In the course of this civil war, more than 140,000 people have been killed, chemical weapons have been used, ancient cities have been decimated and millions of Syrians have fled their country and have become refugees. The war has spilled across the border impacting Lebanon with an influx of refugees, street fights in Tripoli and bombings in Beirut. The official position of the Lebanese government is "non intervention" in Syria. But the Lebanese government isn't the only player in Lebanon.

The Hezbollah Factor:

Hezbollah, an extremist Shiite group, supports the current Assad regime in Syria - as does Iran and Russia. Hezbollah has been a force in Lebanon since 1983 and is lead by Hassan Nasrallah. The group holds to a doctrine of "people,

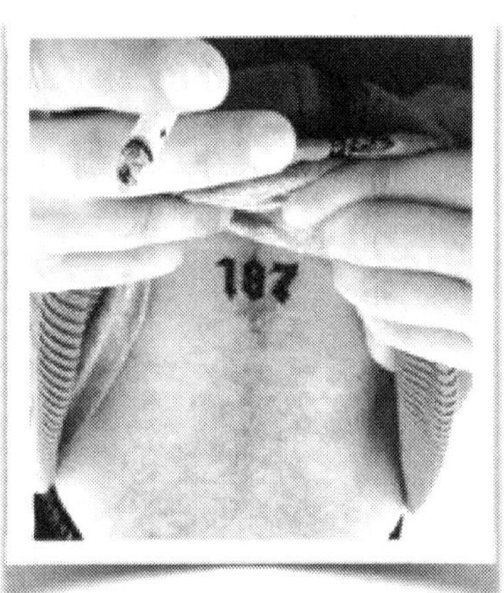

Hezbollah fighter, having just returned from fighting in Syria

plus army, plus resistance" - meaning that it's essential for them to send militants into Syria. This is at odds with the official government "stay out of Syria" policy. Currently there is a significant rift between Hezbollah and Lebanese President Michel Suleiman, especially after recent and unpleasant verbal exchanges have occurred between the two of them.

Mohammad Albouazizi, journalist for the daily political newspaper *Future*, describes Hezbollah's involvement in Syria this way, "Hezbollah claims that they are defending Lebanon and the holy places belonging to the Shiites in Syria. In fact, they are defending the Assad regime, which helps to strengthen their political influence and military presence in Lebanon on religious premises."

Mohamad Balbaki, a Hezbollah fighter who has recently returned from his deployment of fighting in Syria states his view very simply: "When Nasrallah says go fight in Syria, you go. It's that simple."

The Salafist/Sunni Factor

On the other end of the spectrum, you have Salafist and Islamists who have taken control of various neighborhoods in Tripoli, the capital of Lebanon's north. These extremely conservative Sunni Muslims side with the resistance movement in Syria - and against Assad's regime.

Sheikh Khaled Zaaroul.

I recently met with Salafist leader Sheikh Khaled Zaaroul. He denies sending any fighters into the Syrian theater stating that he doesn't want any blood on his hands. He believes that the battle is for ideas, and there is no need for war. His core idea is that of the Umma - the unified Islamic state - a caliphate.

But others close to the situation disagree, saying that the Sheikh is monied, well-connected, influential and action-oriented when it comes to Syria. It is the fear of repercussions from the Lebanese government that cause Salafist leaders to be very fearful of stating their true intentions and actions regarding sending militants into Syria.

When I asked the Sheikh about recent bombings in Beirut, seemingly aimed at Hezbollah targets, he asserted that Hezbollah is bombing itself. He notes that the bombings

mostly take place in areas where there aren't people and that the deaths that have resulted are incidental. Why would Hezbollah do this? According to the Sheikh, they do it to advance the justification for sending fighters into Syria.
To believe this, you have to discount the fact that Abdullah Azzam Brigade, a militant offshoot of al-Qaeda has claimed responsibility for the two largest suicide bombs in Beirut - even issuing a rare apology for the unintended deaths of so many civilians. Other bombings have been claimed by the hard-line Sunni Nusra Front in Lebanon - as revenge against Hezbollah's support for president Assad in Syria.

Sheikh Khaled goes further - claiming that the very existence of Hezbollah is for the protection is Israel. That it was created after the 1982 war with Israel - and since that time Israel and Hezbollah have participated in wars of deception - brief skirmishes that go nowhere and mean nothing. He says that if Hezbollah really believed in the doctrine of resistance, they would not take breaks from resisting the existence and occupation of Israel.

Al-Qaeda Connection

There are some who believe, including the Lebanese intelligence, that the Salafists of Tripoli are connected with al-Qaeda and that there is a growing presence of al-Qaeda in Lebanon. According to Sheikh Khaled Zaaroul, this is not true - but he reduced al-Qaeda to an "idea" more than an organization at this point - mostly because he says there hasn't been an effective al-Qaeda leader since Osama bin Laden. The Sheikh especially admired bin Laden for his ability to bring the "poison to the poisoners." In others words, bin Laden was effective in taking war and destruction to the heart of America, as America had taken war into Muslim lands.

When I asked him about his view of 9/11, he stated that when he first heard and saw the news footage of the attacks he was delighted to see America assaulted in this way. But within five minutes of seeing what happened, he was no longer jubilant. His change of attitude wasn't because of the deaths of thousands of innocent civilians. No, it was because now he realized that the US would have more reasons to justify their war against Muslims.

The Israeli Factor

To the south of Lebanon is the state of Israel. Because of previous wars, occupation issues and the Palestinian matter, Syrian and Lebanon are in a perpetual state of war with Israel. So, what is Israel's current involvement in the Syrian conflict?

According to Radwan Mortada of *Al Akhbar Daily*, Israel is probably hoping that the war continues - happy to watch her enemies destroys themselves. He also believes, in his opinion, that if Israel ever wanted to strike and destroy Hezbollah, now would be the time. Hezbollah's resources are stretched thin because of the Syrian war and, he believes that Hezbollah wouldn't be able to defend themselves against Israeli aggression. Radwan also believes that in the end, Syria will be divided into two states: one for Sunnis and one for Alawites/Shiites. But, he predicts, even with Syria divided, the conflict will continue - and to the benefit of Israel.

Currently, however, Israel is increasingly worried about Iran and its ability to produce a nuclear weapon. Israel is also concerned that the US is developing a closer relationship with Iran and with Hezbollah - an organization that the West has deemed a major terror group. If a closer relationship is being formed, it is obviously over issues of cooperation to minimize Sunni terrorist and al-Qaeda threats, which the US views are more dangerous than Shiite terror policies. Politics and wars make strange bedfellows.

My Lebanese translator, Issa, summed up the conflict with Israel interestingly. According to him, the whole situation with Israel can be traced to one verse in the Quran (17:7) that promises that in the last days, before the appearance of the Mahdi (the Islamic messiah figure), the Jews will enter the Al-Aqsa mosque (on the Temple Mount) for the second time and the mosque will be freed by Muslims. Eschatological worldviews are very powerful motivators. So, as Issa would say, keep fighting against Israel - because your day is coming - your interpretation of the Quran tells you so.

The Impact on Lebanon

In the end, regardless as to the stated government policy that Lebanon will not involve itself in the Syrian conflict, it ***IS*** involved. Whether it likes it admit it or not. Militants are fighting in Syria. Bombs of retribution are going off in Beirut. Tripoli edges closer and closer to a major meltdown. Upwards of a million refugees are now in Lebanon, putting endless strain on Lebanon's already fragile economy. And there is no end in sight.

The U.S. and Afghanistan:
The Next Chapter

Phil Johnson, Ph.D.

From Kabul, Afghanistan

May 29, 2014

US President Obama has made it clear that he plans to withdraw ALL troops from Afghanistan by 2016. After more than a decade of fighting, spending, training and dying, Obama is going to try to keep his vision of ending two wars before he leaves office. (Note, "ending," not necessarily winning.)

The Good News:

We're going to leave about 10,000 troops in Afghanistan for

the time being – as long as we get a security agreement signed with the new leadership of Afghanistan. (Current President, Karzai refuses to sign one.)

The Bad News:

It's bad news to tell our enemies exactly when we're planning to remove all final troops from Afghanistan. It's bad news that bin Laden's death did not mean the end of al-Qaeda. As a result, Afghanistan risks becoming a terrorist haven once again when US and NATO troops leave. It's bad news that the Taliban and al-Qaeda actively recruit new members. And it's bad news that Obama has learned nothing from what happened in Iraq after the US departed.

What will happen:

Brigadier General Feldmann, spokesman for ISAF, whom I interviewed in Kabul in March, feels optimistic. He states that each time he sees an iPhone or iPad in the hands of a young person, it's a boot into the stomach of the Taliban. He feels that modernization and freedom of ideas and thoughts are taking hold. And that's true…with some.

But guess what? The Taliban is still there. The Pakistani Taliban (which may be worse) is still there, straddling the border of Afghanistan and Pakistan. Our ally, the ISI (Pakistan's secret spy service) is supporting the Taliban. (You'd think that $1.7 billion in aid would buy us a better friend!) And the Taliban will continue to undermine the government in Kabul. And they will continue the abusive, repressive treatment of women.

The bottom line is that the Taliban is bent upon instituting a 7th century version of Sharia Law on the entire country. (And not a version that every Muslim believes is a true representation of Islamic faith.) And I don't believe that the Afghan forces are ready to go it alone against them. Not yet. (Not to mention the possibility of a national war that could break out once the troops leave.)

Sure, it's tough being America. It seems unfair to have to police the world and sacrifice lives and treasure to try to protect ourselves (and the world) from people stuck in the 7th century. But what's the alternative? Should Afghans be responsible for their own nation? Yes. Are they ready to do that right now with no help? No.

Ideas, like those of the Taliban, are not influenced by negotiations or trade deals. They do not hold opinions that can simply be debated. They have "ideals" that drive behavior with a fervor that only radicalized religion can create. Author James Fergusson offers this quote from his interviews with a Taliban member, "One year, a hundred years, a million years, ten million years — it is not important. We will never stop fighting. At Judgment Day, Allah will not ask, 'What did you do for your country.' He will ask, 'Did you fight for your religion?'"

For the sake of Afghan's neighborhood, for the sake of the West and for the sake of the Afghan people, I think we need to leave enough troops behind to make sure we finish what we started and don't lose more than a decade of gain. But chances are, we won't. And chances are the Taliban will resurge, violence will increase and more lives will be lost.

Five for One

The Taliban Prisoner Trade

Phil Johnson, Ph.D.

From Frisco, Texas, USA

June 9, 2014

Americans and the media have been buzzing this past week about the latest issue in Obama's attempt to manage America's foreign policy and end the war in Afghanistan while not completely ruining his political career in the process. **Here's what happened:**

US soldier, Bowe Bergdahl, was held prisoner by the Taliban in Afghanistan for 5 years. President Obama, without alerting Congress, made a prisoner exchange deal that returned five top Taliban guys who had been held in

Guantanamo prison for the last dozen years or so for Bergdahl. The Taliban-Five were transferred to Doha, Qatar where their movements will be restricted for a year. There are lots of opinions on both sides of this issue ranging from "We must do anything possible to never leave an American behind," to "The President broke the law by not informing Congress of the prisoner swap." So…

Here are 7 things you need to know about the situation:

1. **Bergdahl was a deserter.** That is pretty much without question based on reports from those who were with him and served with him. Did he collaborate with the enemy? We don't know yet.

2. **It's not a good trade.** These Taliban guys were turned over to Qatar – and are supposed to be restricted for a year. Even so, we need to remember, these guys are not just soldiers that were captured during a war – they are criminals of war, guilty of crimes against humanity. They might be in their 40's now, but I doubt their ideals have changed. They will eventually go back to Afghanistan and to the "cause."

3. **The Taliban is not the legitimate government of Afghanistan – so why are we negotiating with them?** The Taliban is not a "government in exile." Afghanistan has a president and a government (a corrupt one, to be sure). The

Afghans recently had a presidential election. When the final run-off is complete, they will have experienced the first peaceful transfer (elected) president in their history.

4. Qatar (where the former Taliban prisoners were sent) seems to be becoming a haven for the dangerous. According to the *National Post,* "Moussa Koussa, the ex-spy chief of former Libyan dictator Col. Muammar Gaddafi; Khaled Meshaal, the head of Hamas' political Bureau; and influential Muslim cleric Sheikh Yousuf Al-Qaradawi are just some of the characters who can be found sipping tea in the Four Seasons hotel in Doha." (**National Post**)

5. Jihadist membership and activity is increasing. According to the Rand Institute's National Defense Research Institute, since 2010, the number of Jihadist groups across North Africa and the Middle East has increased 58%. Radicalism is growing. It has become decentralize and more effective. (**Jihadist Group Study**)

6. America may choose to leave Afghanistan in 2016 – but the Taliban will not give up – nor will they change. The US has spent $50 billion on preparing Afghan security forces – but according to military experts, those forces aren't even close to being ready yet. The Center for Strategic and International Studies says, "The training program has been "rushed forward" to meet an artificially-imposed deadline, and that the Afghans may not be ready to stand on their own before 2018." (**Foreign Policy**)

7. It's not just US citizens that are upset about this trade. Many Afghans are also angry. This latest move by the US president sends a message – and that message is that the US is ready to completely disengage from what we've spent more than a decade trying to build in Afghanistan.

Nation building is hard – and as they say, "generational" – meaning that most of us won't see lasting change in our lifetimes. And maybe we haven't seen the kind of success that we wanted in creating a desirable national infrastructure in places like Iraq and Afghanistan. I certainly don't have the answers for all of this. But one thing I do know- the answer isn't in releasing murderers back into action.

Ukraine, Russia, Gaza and Israel: Are there Two Sides to Every Story?

Phil Johnson, Ph.D.
From Kiev, Ukraine
July 20, 2014

Ukrainian police massed against Ukrainian protestors.

July 17th was a bad day, to say the least. Malaysian Airline flight 17 was shot down over Ukraine and after 10 days of rockets and airstrikes between Gaza and Israel, Israel began a ground invasion into Gaza. A lot of people have died. Many more have had their lives turned upside down.

There will be lots of continuing media coverage and lots of debates about what happened and who's at fault. People will express their opinions and regardless as to the availability of information, people rarely change their pre-existing viewpoints. So at the very least, we can attempt to understand the motivations behind what's currently going on in the world. Here's a quick look:

RUSSIA AND UKRAINE:

In February I was in Ukraine when demonstrations against the government were heating up. The issue: Will Ukraine stay in lockstep with Russia or will they move towards the European Union? The protesters were in favor of freedom to determine their own future and to enter into a closer relationship with Europe. Since my visit, things have only gotten worse and if people weren't paying attention before, with the shooting down of a passenger plane and the death of almost 300 people, what's happening between Ukraine and Russia is now definitely in the "awareness zone" of most people.

Russia's Motivation:

I'm pretty sure that the downing of the Malaysian passenger plane was not intentional. That would have served no one's interests. It was most likely a horrible miscalculation with unimaginable, horrific consequences. It is yet to be determined how involved Russia was in the shooting down of MH17, but it's pretty clear that Russia is involved in stirring up and aiding pro-Russian insurgents in Ukraine.

The reason – as you will find with almost all international conflict – is the protection of national rights or interests. Russia does not want the buffer zone of Ukraine – their safety zone between Russia and NATO nations – to be erased. They want regional influence and intend to expand it. Russia doesn't want Ukraine leaning towards Europe and NATO any more than the US likes the idea of Russia reinstating intelligence facilities in Cuba.

Ukraine's Motivation:

Ukraine, on the other hand, wants the freedom to move towards the European Union and doesn't want Russia interfering in their country, limiting their future opportunities or inciting unrest in the more Russia-leaning eastern part of the country. At the moment, Ukraine has lost Crimea, and is in danger of having their country split in two.

ISRAEL AND GAZA

And then there is the continuing conflict between Gaza and Israel. I have been to Israel many times, as well as to the West Bank (or Palestinian Territory). I have also been to the border between Israel and Gaza and have interviewed a top Hamas official in his Damascus office. Here are the basic worldviews of each group:

Gaza's Motivation:

This is not necessarily the view of all Palestinian people, at least not the ones I have spoken to. This is really Hamas' worldview, the current government of Gaza and an offshoot of the Muslim Brotherhood. Hamas firmly believes that Israel has no right to exist, that they have stolen the land from the Palestinian people and that they continue to oppress, imprison and kill Palestinians. Israelis are the terrorists and the aggressors. Hamas' primary motivation is to destroy Israel and reclaim what they feel is rightfully theirs.

They want the release of political prisoners and an end of blockades. They are not necessarily interested in peace or in negotiating. They recently refused the cease fire agreement that Egypt helped negotiate and that Israelis accepted. But that is consistent with Hamas' worldview. They view themselves as freedom fighters. Even in my interview several years ago with Talal Nasser, spokesman for Hamas in their former Damascus office, I was told that Hamas will do whatever it takes to wipe Israel off the map and will not give up on that goal until it is accomplished.

Unfortunately, because of this worldview, many innocent Palestinians have died. Even Egypt's foreign minister (not usually a fan of Israel) blamed Hamas for more Palestinian deaths because of their refusal to accept the ceasefire agreement.

Israel's Motivation:

Israel's motivation is national survival and security for its citizens. They believe that they have the right to exist and have the right to defend her borders. Hundreds of rockets were fired into Israel before Israel responded to Gaza. Israel's goal is to strike Hamas' weapon stockpiles and rocket capabilities – and it would be nice if Hamas didn't use civilians as human shields. Israel notifies Palestinian civilians before they make airstrikes so they can evacuate the specific targeted area. And while Israel feels that she is held to a higher standard than other nations, it doesn't change the fact that innocent people are killed during the airstrikes – intentionally or not.

While Israel accepted Egypt's ceasefire agreement, they resumed attacks when Hamas continued to fire rockets into Israel. When 13 Hamas militants emerged from a tunnel on the Israeli side of the border, Israel decided it was time for a ground invasion with the stated goals of destroying Hamas' tunnels and its ability to strike Israel with missiles.

Thinking it Through:

There is much more that can be said on each side of all viewpoints. There are facts, there are biases, there are core beliefs, there is willful denial – much more than can be written about in a simple blog or article. Firmly held beliefs are not likely to change – and people tend to look for and absorb information that supports what they already believe.

How you feel about Russia and the Ukraine or your views on Israel and Gaza may or may not change with time and information. But if you find yourself unable to articulate the "other guy's" viewpoint or motivation, then you should reevaluate your thinking skills and seek additional perspectives and comprehensive information. Admitting that we might not have all the facts or all the answers is a good step in beginning to understand complex global situations.

Israel and Gaza: Spin City

Phil Johnson, Ph.D.
From Frisco, Texas, USA
August 8, 2014

The ceasefire between Gaza and Israel is over and rockets are flying from both sides now. According to the *New York Times,* Hamas broke the temporary peace just before the expiration of the 72-hour ceasefire. During negotiations in Cairo, **Hamas declared** that the fighting wouldn't end until their demands were met. A spokesman for the military wing of Hamas said: "Our demands are purely humanitarian and need no negotiations because it is the right of human beings to live."

The Israeli-Gaza Conflict is all over the media, but the reporting is anything but comprehensive and clear. The narratives on both sides of the issue are completely different and emotions have become more powerful than information.

On the Israeli side, it is all about defending their right to exist and their right to security. But there is not a lot of talk about settlements, unreleased political prisoners and the fact that Gaza's borders are closed, preventing freedom of movement, imports and medical care for Palestinians.

On the Gaza side, the narrative is all about fighting for their freedom and destroying the "occupiers." There is no discussion about the reason behind the closing of Gaza's borders. Both Israel and Egypt know that with open borders, more weapons will flow into Gaza from Iran and will be used against Gaza's neighbors. There is no talk about Hamas using civilians as human shields, knowing that lots of dead Palestinian civilians are a powerful propaganda weapon against Israel.

This past week, I spoke to two of my contacts: one inside Gaza and one inside Israel.

My Palestinian contact exhibited high spirits as he spoke about the 40 people now living in his house – because they have nowhere else to go. He spoke of what they are doing to survive and his confidence that the Palestinians were actually giving Israel a good beating in this battle. He told me he used to hate Hamas, but now he loves them. Regarding using human shields? He says, "Of course not – no one would ever do that." (Note: Even the UN has verified that weapons have been placed in UNRWA schools. And Indian TV and French TV have provided videos showing how Hamas fires rockets from populated areas – much to the consternation of Hamas.)

My Israeli contact was more philosophical expressing the frustration with the loss of life on both sides. But he recognized the inevitability of casualties if Hamas continued to target Israeli civilians with rockets. He also expressed his confusion over the US's lack of support – and the US's alliance with Turkey and Qatar, even while Egypt and Saudi Arabia were more supportive of Israel.

So, in the middle of all that's going on, and given the obvious bias and spin in much of the media (on all sides) – where do you turn for information? Here are a few names that I think exhibit intelligence, balance and context. Look them up and see what they have to say on this issues (and many other issues.)

1. **Dr. Zuhdi Jasser** is the President of the American Islamic Forum for Democracy. He is a devout, observant Muslim who is a thoughtful defender of freedom and truth. (http://aifdemocracy.org)

2. **Dr. Walid Phares**, is a professor and author. He also advises the US House of Representatives on Middle East issues. (walidphares.com)

3. **Dr. Charles Krauthammer**, is a columnist for *The Washington Post*, a contributor to the *Weekly Standard*, as well as a media commentator and author. He is simply one of the most articulate, smartest guys I know. (Just google him – he's got lots of articles out there that are worth reading.)

While I rarely agree with everything anyone says – hopefully these suggestions will be a place to start gathering information on very complex and very important topic!

Happiness Factor:
Who's Happy and Why?

Phil Johnson, Ph.D.
October 3, 2014
From Copenhagen, Denmark

Are you happy? Would you know it if you were? How would you actually define happiness? The founding fathers of America bothered to include the "pursuit of happiness" as one of the inalienable rights of all humans. Of course, the right to "pursue" happiness is not necessarily a guarantee of finding happiness.

But according to the latest *World Happiness Report,* a few countries seem to have managed to discover happiness - and topping that list is Denmark. According to the report, "happiness" was measured based on the level that a nation enjoyed social support, freedom to make life choices, generosity, perceptions of corruption, life expectancy and GDP per capita. On a scale from 1 to 10, Denmark scored a 7.693, followed closely by Norway (7.655), Switzerland (7.650), Netherlands (7.512) and Sweden (7.480). While happiness is something that people talk about, evaluate and chase, I was intrigued as to how people would define it and what - if anything - they would give up to achieve it. So, I was off to Copenhagen to find out just what it was that the Danes had discovered and to see if they were as happy as the recent data suggested.

The Heart of Hygge

One of the first Danish concepts that I heard about was "*hygge.*" The Danes will tell you that there is no exact English translation for the word, but generally, it means "coziness." (By the way, when people around the world tell me that they have words, values, or concepts that cannot be translated into English, it makes me want to spout off English words that also are never "exactly"

translatable into other languages, like “entrepreneur,” “stuff” or “Black-Friday Sales.”)

Hygge is that sense of closeness, warmth and belonging that helps sustain Danes through the long dark winters. And through difficult times. Add some good food and candles and it’s part of the social support that Danes enjoy that contributes to their perception of being “happy.” But when I spoke to immigrants who were trying to make a new life in Denmark, they expressed that this “Danish happiness” was a bit illusive for them. Apparently finding *hygge* is not so easy if Denmark is your adopted country. Sanjay, from India, has been in Denmark for more than a year. Is he happy? Not yet. He says that it’s been hard to break in to society and that it took him a long time to make friends. The friends he has made are other immigrants.

The Freedom Factor

High on the list of factors that indicate happiness and satisfaction is the freedom to make choices. So, it seemed like the place to check out “freedom of choice” was Christiania also knows as the Freetown of Christiania - a little enclave of Copenhagen that doesn’t actually believe that they are part of Denmark - or the European Union for that matter. They are a self-proclaimed autonomous neighborhood that started in 1971. As an anything-goes-community, they have been shut down, reopened, raided by police and remain a source of controversy. Cannabis is openly sold and used here and to a large degree, has been tolerated by the authorities. Sort of.

Would I find more happiness here? There seemed to be expanded “freedoms” in this neighborhood, so I assumed I might find more “happiness.”

The first person I spoke to was Trina. She is an artist. Painting puts her in a good mood. Smoking marijuana puts her in a better mood. Me and my questions definitely did not put her in a good mood. To be fair, she was busy putting together a luncheon, had paintings to attend to and her joint wasn’t going to roll itself. A nosey journalist did not add to her quality of life.

Jannik, a young shop owner told me that the government in Denmark provides well for the people - which meant that he could provide well for his “extracurricular” activities. But recently he realized that in addition to government support, he would have to get a job. That did not make him happy.

Moustafa Petersen, a 19 year-old half Moroccan - half Danish student, told me that his definition of happiness was a good party. And yes, he was happy to have free education and security from the government. But he was mostly happy for parties.

The one thing all these residents of Christiania had in common was the answer to this question: *"Given the wealth of your country, your relative security, your freedom of choices and opportunities - how would you most like your life to be remembered?"*

The answer was always the same from this group of people: *"I don't need to be remembered for anything."* For them, happiness was for the moment - and lasted no longer than the day, the party or the money in their pockets.

Happiness or Security?

Simon Christiansen, photojournalist.

But Christiania is just a small slice of life in Denmark. I was sure there were other perspectives, so I turned to my friend Simon Christiansen, a photojournalist in Copenhagen who works for Berlingske Media. Simon and I had both done some journalistic work in Lebanon in the past, so I knew he had seen other parts of the world - less secure parts of the world. I was eager to hear what he thought about happiness.

I told Simon that the more I spoke with people in Denmark and the more I looked into the factors that determined which countries and which people were happy, I couldn't help but see a consistent trend. People were ranked happier when their government provided more security.

Does security equal happiness? Do you think that's accurate?

"Personally for Danish people, life is really simple. The Danish community and the welfare is such a good foundation for being happy - free education, good social support. But there is also a concept in Danish culture called "jante" which tells us to be humble, not to promote yourself, don't try to be better than others and to keep your expectations reasonable."

To me that sounded more like security and contentment - which are great things - but not exactly happiness. The principle of "*jante*" might teach people contentment and a limit, but not really happiness. What about ambition? What about risk? What about fulfillment?

Should life have deeper meaning and fulfillment?

"Personal fulfillment is very important for my happiness. I try not to obsess about it, but so far, things have gone well. I admit that it can become a bit boring if everything is working out. You don't have anything to risk...no chances to take - things become dull."

What about religion? Does that play a role in someone's happiness?

"Denmark is a Christian, secularized country. I am not religious, but I don't exclude it. Personally, religion does not play a role in my happiness. But I do feel that I have a lot of faith and spirituality. God equals the universe. I like to delve into my inner world through nature or meditation. There is as much to be found in the inner world as in the outer world."

What if the world changes? What if what seems stable now becomes unstable? Where will the source of your happiness come from when all of this security is gone?

"There would definitely be more pressure, it might make me a bit more career minded and serious, but I think I would still keep my same values - to contribute, to help and to volunteer."

Lars Rievers, an editor at Berlingske Media and co-worker of Simon echoes similar sentiments. He believes that happiness can be found in friends and family. He also believes that doing work that "*makes sense and matters*" also contributes to happiness.

When I asked Lars if he thinks that government programs and security add to happiness, he told me "*not completely.*" He went on to explain that he has family in the United States. He said that when his mother (in Denmark) is ill or needs care, he calls the government and tells them to take care of it. His family in the US tells him that when their parents or family members have problems, they don't call the government, they rely on family and friends to help. He says, *"There is something right about doing it that way - that personal commitment to taking care of our own. There might be some happiness in that as well."*

I asked Lars is he would trade security and accept risk if it added more meaning to his life?

"Yes, at this point in my life - yes. But I think that people at different seasons of their life would answer that question differently. Right now I have less to lose - so I can afford to take more risk."

Simon Christiansen agreed that deeper meaning would be worth the risk. So, how does Simon, a single guy in his 20's, brimming with potential, want to be remembered 100 years from now?

"I want to be remembered for my attitude and my presence. I want to be remembered as a person who was very devoted and who took responsibility for the things I want, rather than complaining and worrying about it. I want to be remembered for being optimistic."

Genetic Optimism

Ah, the "Danish Optimism." There is actually a theory about that too. Researchers from the University of Warwick evaluated information from 131 countries and found that the closer a nation was genetically to the Danes, the happier its people were. In summary, when it comes to the gene that is linked to low levels of life satisfaction, fewer Danes possess this version of the gene - and therefore are not as susceptible to depression or unhappiness.

And that might end up being really important - because as most of us have figured out, the world is not stable and security is an illusion. The pursuit of happiness may have a head start when you live in a wealthy, stable, socially-oriented nation - but it doesn't guarantee the kind of happiness that resonates in your soul and that exists regardless as to your circumstances or geographic location. That kind of enduring happiness requires a life of meaning, purpose and the pursuit of fulfillment - and it is "location independent." That sort of abiding happiness often includes risk and getting out of one's comfort zone.

True happiness, I believe, involves living for something outside yourself, bigger than yourself and it doesn't always come with guaranteed security - or even a guaranteed successful outcome. But that's life - and a good life doesn't just consist of an easy existence. But if you are fortunate enough to have the advantages of wealth, security and friends - I think the world expect deeper attempts at living bigger and experiencing deeply fulfilling happiness - not just static existence. But don't worry too much about happiness and the state of the world - my optimistic Danish friends will tell you, "everything will work out OK." They're just happy like that.

The ISIS Threat: As Viewed from Lebanon

Phil Johnson, Ph.D.
From Beirut, Lebanon
October 9, 2014

Regardless as to the US-led airstrikes which began several weeks ago, ISIS remains on the march. As I write this, the strategic town of Kobani, on Syria's border with Turkey, is under siege. It seems likely now that Kobani may fall to ISIS - and Turkey seems to sit on the border with tanks, but does nothing. *Time.com* put it this way, "If the ISIS militants take control of Kobani, they will have a huge strategic corridor along the Turkish border, linking with the terrorist group's positions in Aleppo to the west and Raqqa to the east."

A few days ago in Beirut, I sat down with Radwan Mortada, an investigative journalist for *Al Akbar English* and noted expert on terrorism and terrorist groups in the Middle East. Here's what we talked about:

Lebanon borders Syria - you've already had a border town temporarily taken over by ISIS militants. What is the general view of ISIS in Lebanon?

Most are afraid. They think they will go to sleep and wake up with a nightmare. But in the mind of ISIS, Lebanon is already a part of Syria – they already consider us to be part of the Islamic State.

In August, the Islamic militants took the town of Arsal – a border town in the north of Lebanon. Thirty-eight soldiers were kidnapped. Some have been assassinated. The return of others has been negotiated. Some are still held hostage. The media will tell you that the Lebanese army has retaken the town – but ISIS and al Nusra Front (another militant group in the Islamic State) come and go as they like.

The real dangers are now for Jordan, Saudi Arabia and Kuwait. Those are the countries in the sights of ISIS and al Nusra Front now.

How big a threat is ISIS to the region and the world?

Radwan Mortada of Al-Akhbar English

When the U.S. started their air strikes, they began to target al Nusra Front, not ISIS forces. It's because the US thinks al Nusra Front is more dangerous than ISIS. Al Nusra Front is the arm of al Qaeda in Iraq and Syria and this is the group that is most likely to strike the West. Most likely to strike the West from inside the West.

Both ISIS and al Nusra Front want the same thing - the want an Islamic Caliphate. ISIS uses killing as propaganda. They post their mass killings and beheadings on social media. Al Nusra Front is guilty of the same violent actions, but they have stopped advertising what they're doing. They realized that posting a beheading scared the West, but it also scared off potential recruits for the movement. Al Nusra Front are playing a smarter, more subtle PR game now. Ultimately they will prove to be more effective at recruiting new members and radicalizing them. They will prove to be more dangerous.

If ISIS and al Nusra Front have the same goal, why are they not united?

They were united and working together. But the division between the two groups is personal - it's between the two leaders, al-Baghdadi (ISIS) and al-Julani (Al Nusra Front). The two groups will not be united until one of those leaders is dead. And they are actively trying to kill one another.

Is the US-led campaign proving effective in deterring the militants?

What I can tell you is this, the US will eventually need to put troops on the ground in Iraq and Syria if they want success. It won't happen with just airstrikes.

I have a journalist contact in Syria who tells me that once the airstrikes from the West started, the strategy of ISIS became to melt into the general population. The hope is that the US will follow them, bomb populated areas and unintentionally kill many civilians in the process. This, they believe, will promote the cause for the Islamic State and unite people against that West. What do you think?

Yes, they are doing this – and this will definitely increase efforts to recruit fighters. It simply increases membership locally and from foreign fighters. Already the airstrikes themselves are helping to increase membership. Another reason that ISIS will be difficult to defeat is that they are the people now, not just a militant group.

What impact, if any, is ISIS and al Nusra Front having on Israel, which also borders Syria?

Two towns near Syria's border with Israel, Dar'a and al Qunaytirah are currently controlled by al Nusra Front. At the present time, they won't do anything against Israel because they feel they are too young and don't want to take that risk until they are stronger and more prepared. But if they did a strike on Israel (and there is some pressure for this group to take action) that would put them on the map and increase recruitment to a large degree. It would make al

Nusra Front more attractive than ISIS in the eyes of the people.

Radwan also told me that recent intelligence reports indicate that attacks were likely inside Lebanon in the days to come – most likely coming from the Abdallah Azzam brigade, a Lebanese radical group. Radwan says that the target is the Lebanese army and Hezbollah, potentially creating more instability in already fragile Lebanon.

In the bigger picture, 60 countries have signed on to the coalition to halt the Islamic State from their continued advances in Syria and Iraq. To be sure, many of the allied nations are simply providing political support, humanitarian aid, supplies or training for Kurdish fighters. Recently, Iran offered material support to the country of Lebanon to help keep ISIS at bay. The Lebanese have mixed feelings about Iran's offer – but as Radwan would say, we'll take help from wherever it comes. The question now is this: Can ISIS and other associated militants be defeated (or at least be significantly degraded) or is it too little too late?

Rome, Qatar and Chasing Rabbits

Phil Johnson, Ph.D.

From Doha, Qatar

November 24, 2014

I recently returned from conducting a leadership conference in Italy followed by some research work in Qatar – two very different places, and each with a unique voice in the world.

Rome is the home of the Roman Catholic Church and Pope Francis (who was recently ranked as the 4th most powerful person in the world according to *Forbes Magazine*). Qatar, is a Muslim-majority state and home to *Al Jazeera,* one of the most powerful global voices in media – influencing millions.

As different as these two places are, they do have something in common – ***an on-going identity crisis.*** Neither place seems to know who they are. Consider the following:

- Rome is the epicenter of Catholic Christianity with 2000 years of tradition to lean on – but a recent survey found that in areas of abortion, premarital sex and same-sex marriage, US and European Catholics are more liberal than the teachings of the church. The Catholic church is clear on moral integrity – and yet even in Rome, it seems that few connect what they believe with how they live and behave.

- Qatar suffers from their own form of an identity crisis. They are a small nation with lots of oil-money. They are supposedly an ally of the US and yet they abet terrorism. They host the largest US military base in the Middle East (which provides them with a significant measure of security in the region). At the same time, they have allowed private fundraising for al-Qaeda and

> ISIS and they have courted the friendship of the Muslim Brotherhood and Salafist groups (which gives them the perception of regional influence – especially as a counterbalance to Saudi Arabia).

In an interview with CNN's Christiane Amanpour, the new emir of Qatar responded to this apparent duplicity with the following statement: *"I'm not in a camp against another camp. ... I have my own way of thinking."* Which simply means, *"I'm going to sit on the fence, not decide who I'm going to be, and hope that it all works out."*

And it won't. It never does. No one can stay on the fence forever. You cannot call yourself a follower of Christ and act nothing like Him. You cannot call yourself a friend of one country while funding their enemies. Everyone…every nation…every group…every individual has to eventually decide who they are, choose their path and live with the consequences – for better or worse. The middle is not an option. The middle isn't fair to yourself, to those around you and the "middle" never leads anywhere productive.

The Russians have a very good proverb about this very thing. They say, *"If you chase two rabbits, you will not catch either one."*

ISIS: Fire and the Healing of the Believer's Chest

Phil Johnson, Ph.D.
February 6, 2015
From Frisco, Texas USA

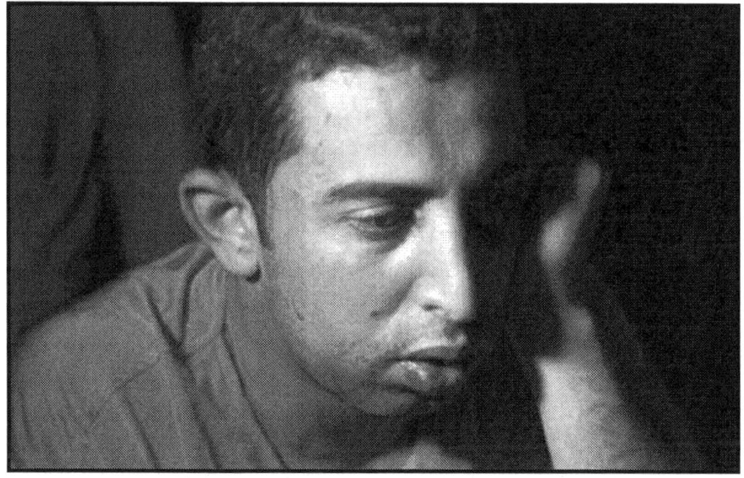

Over the last couple of weeks, ISIS (Islamic State) has continued to make headlines by gaining territory in Syria, decapitating two Japanese journalists and releasing a highly-produced video showing the burning alive of Jordanian pilot, Muath al-Kassasbeh.

In addition, a report released on Wednesday by the U.N. Committee on the Rights of the Child said it had received reports regarding ISIS of "several cases of mass executions of boys, as well as reports of beheadings, crucifixions of children and burying children alive." As questions about ISIS, radical Islam and the world's response continue to grow, I thought we should address a couple of issues:

Does the Koran condone burning people alive?

With all the atrocities being committed, it seems that the horrific burning death of Jordan's pilot has managed to gain the world's attention – and collective horror. The title of the video showing the burning of the pilot alive is entitled, "Healing the Believer's Chests." The title of the video, according to the *Observer*, comes from the Koran 9:14, *"fight them and Allah will punish them by your hands, cover them with shame, help you over them, heal the breasts of Believers."*

In general, according to the *Observer*, burning someone alive is reserved for someone who has betrayed Islam – and that is what ISIS believes the young pilot from Jordan has done. But many Muslims say that burning one's enemies or prisoners of war is prohibited by Islam. The head of Sunni Islam's respected university, **Egypt's Al-Azhar,** described the ISIS militants as "enemies of God and the Prophet Mohamed."

Is Islam a radical religion?

I know a lot of Muslims. Some are good friends. Some have worked for me and contributed in meaningful ways to my organization. These people and the vast majority of other Muslims are not radicalized or violent. They want peace and they exhibit tolerance for a world that holds many beliefs and viewpoints.

But it would be naive to think that there is no radical, extreme element in Islam. And I don't think it's just a "few fringe" people. It turns out that "radicalism" is sometimes in the eye of the beholder. After all, for some Muslims, it's just about being faithful and obedient to what God's Word (the Koran) has prescribed. Ahmed al-Tayed, grand imam of Al-Azhar University, says that ISIS deserves "the Koran-prescribed punished of death: crucifixion, or the chopping off of their arms." He goes on to say, "Islam prohibits the taking of an innocent life."

But many lives have been taken in the name of Islam, and not just by ISIS. (I think of the recent murders of *Charlie Hebdo* employees in Paris, suicide bombings in Afghanistan, the murder of children in Pakistan by the Taliban, the kidnappings and abuse of children by Boko Haram and much more.) Who is deciding who is "innocent or who is guilty?" ISIS didn't view the Jordanian pilot as "innocent," since his plane was shot down during a bombing raid on ISIS positions.

There are a large number of people in Muslim-majority

countries who believe that their nation should be run as a "theocracy" – a country governed by the principles of God, as laid out in the Koran. The rub comes when that "final source of truth" is interpreted. And there are many different views on how the Koran and the Hadiths would or should be interpreted and applied.

A *Pew Research Study* in 2013 reveals some of the thinking inside the Muslim faith. Here are just a few of the responses to the survey:

Percentage of people who say that Sharia Law should be the "law of the land."

- Malaysia: 86%
- Afghanistan: 99%
- Pakistan: 84%
- Iraq: 91%
- Egypt: 74%
- Jordan: 71%

Percentage of people who say that corporal punishment should be applied to thieves. (Of those who believe Sharia Law should be the "law of the land.")

- Malaysia: 66%
- Afghanistan: 81%

- Pakistan: 88%
- Iraq: 56%
- Egypt: 70%
- Jordan: 57%

Percentage of people who say that the death penalty should be applied to those who leave Islam. (Of those who believe Sharia Law should be the "law of the land.")

- Malaysia: 62%
- Afghanistan: 79%
- Pakistan: 76%
- Iraq: 42%
- Egypt: 86%
- Jordan: 82%

How should the world respond?

The big question being thrown around now is "Whose war is this?" Is it a US war? A Western war? A Regional war? A Muslim war? In the middle of unspeakable acts of cruelty and immediate danger to Christians, Muslims and other religious minorities, people are somehow bringing up the Crusades and the Inquisition as if to say, "all religions have had their problems." And then there's the favorite "blame-based" argument: "…if the US had never gone into Iraq in the first place…"

Well, you can't unscramble an egg – what's done is done. And referencing the bad behavior of groups that happened hundreds or thousands of years ago is childish as a deflective-based argument. The question now should be: "What can we do to stop these monsters from continuing their killings, torture and abuse in the name of Islam." And like it or not, they are doing it in the name of Allah, in the misguided attempt to please him. But for now, it is everyone's war.

Paris: The Charlie Hebdo Effect Still Lingers

Phil Johnson, Ph.D.
From Paris, France
March 2, 2015

I just finished a leadership conference in Germany and Italy and arrived in Paris last night- a place that was awash in terror on January 7th when the offices of *Charlie Hebdo,* a French satirical magazine was attacked. Two days later, a kosher (Jewish) market in the south-eastern area of Paris was attacked. In the end, 17 people were killed and Paris is still recovering from the tragedy.

Tomorrow, a new group of Global Next students begins their journey to Paris for a leadership conference, ironically enough, on the topic of communication skills. So we will undoubtedly discuss freedom of expression, freedom of thought, freedom to criticize, freedom to offend and all the values, consequences and responsibilities of that freedom.

Paris now seems like the perfect place to have those discussions.

In addition to visiting the site of the *Charlie Hebdo* shootings today, I also sat down at lunch with two French Jews (neither of whom wished to be named in this post) to discuss growing anti-Semitism in Europe. Between recent events in France, angst in Israel and all the controversy surrounding

Israeli Prime Minister Benjamin Netanyahu speaking to the US Congress this week about the threat of a nuclear Iran, I was interested to hear the thoughts of European Jews. Here are the highlights:

Regarding Israeli Prime Minister Benjamin Netanyahu: My two lunch guests believe he runs Israel more like a "king" than a prime minister. They are not fans.

Regarding President Obama: They think that he's incredibly weak and Putin is making a fool of him. They attribute absolutely no leadership to the American president.

Regarding Iran: They believe that Iran is not just a problem for Israel, it's a problem for the world. They reminded me that when Israel bombed the Osiris nuclear facility (a nuclear reactor purchased from France) outside of Baghdad in 1981, (3 weeks before Israeli elections...hmmm...) no one was certain of what the reaction or consequences would be. There were lots of UN meetings and resolutions and condemnations of Israel's actions -but that's about it. And in Israel's view, a nuclear Iraq was avoided – and a message was sent. Therefore, if Israel should respond militarily to Iran's nuclear program, the world also can't predict the outcome – or suggest that Israel not act in its own interests. (But I'm pretty sure the response this time around would be much greater than Iraq's response – and not just through the UN and global condemnation.)

Regarding Netanyahu's call for all European Jews to immigrate to Israel: He's right, both men agreed – Europe is not safe for Jews. One of the men mentioned that he will not – cannot – live in a country where his son could be beaten on the street simply because of who he is.

The Jewish perspective is not the only one in France at this time – there is a growing concern for Muslims too. Karim, an Egyptian immigrant I spoke to viewed the Paris shootings (perpetrated by Muslim extremists) through a different lens – the lens of "what does the world think of me and my faith." He hates his faith being identified with violent and radical behavior. And while he deeply disagrees with and is offended by the caricatures produced by *Charlie Hebdo*, he is also offended by how these acts of violence change the way the world sees his faith – a faith, he says, that is not represented by hate and extremism.

ISIS: The Kurdish Factor

Phil Johnson, Ph.D.
From Erbil, Iraq
March 21, 2015

Me and Peshmerga soldiers near the Gwer front in Iraq.

Today is Kurdish Newroz - a celebration of the Kurdish New Year. This year, the celebration coincides with yesterday's release of a graphic video produced by ISIS showing the brutal beheadings of three Kurdish Peshmerga soldiers. At least 14 other soldiers are still being held hostage. Global Next's sources inside Iraq indicate that the remaining hostages may very well be burned alive.

Last week I was in Iraq tracking the continuing and horrific story of ISIS and their continued assault on, well, just about everyone who is not THEM. I went to northern Iraq, to the Kurdistan region to meet Peshmerga forces near the frontline in Gwer. I wanted to talk with those who are involved first-hand in the battle against ISIS. So let's break it down: Where is Gwer, who are the Peshmerga fighters and who did I speak to?

PESHMERGA

The word literally means "one who confronts death." The Peshmerga are the military forces of Iraqi Kurdistan - they are known for their bravery and their direct, committed confrontation with the forces of the Islamic State (ISIS).

GWER -

Gwer, in Mosul province, is 45 kilometers (about 27 miles) from Erbil, the capital of Iraqi Kurdistan. It is one of the active fronts against ISIS. While there is armed conflict here every day, the most recent heavy attacks occurred on February 9th and left heavy casualties for ISIS. As many as twenty Peshmerga soldiers were also killed, according to Commander Jamal Mutka. As I was told by head Commander Mutka, the Kurds had no intention of letting ISIS gain control over Gwer - which could lead to the fall of Erbil. ISIS was pushed back after about three hours of intense fighting.

Mr. (Hakim) Jamal

Mr. Jamal is a high-ranking lawyer and the second in command of the Peshmerga forces in Gwer. He is also in charge of media relations for the Kurdish forces.

In our conversation, he estimated the number of ISIS fighters in Iraq at 10,000. He is frustrated by the lack of US support and says the Kurdish forces need weapons. So far there has been no direct supplies given to the Kurds, only airstrike support - and that only goes so far.

As Hakim Jamal says, "We are fighting ISIS not as Peshmerga, but as representatives of all humanity." He also expressed discouragement over the fact that the US appears to be more interested in helping its enemies than in helping its friends. The Kurds consider themselves to be great friends and great supporters of the United States. He cited the example that the US is directly helping the Shiite Muslims of the Iraqi government who, in the past, have done everything they could possibly do against the US. He stated that Germany, France, and Italy have helped much more than America, based on his experience in this fight.

He went on to say, "Iran calls Americans devil worshippers, but the US is more supportive towards Iran than they are towards the Kurdish people."

When I asked him if he believes that Turkey is supporting ISIS, his response was, "America knows the answer to this questions so maybe you should ask them." (There have been many reports of Turkey allowing passage of people across their border to join ISIS.) He continued, "America draws the map for all the world. Kurdistan considers themselves a friend of America. Why doesn't America stand up for Kurdistan freedom?"

Mr. Jamal believes that without US help, the Kurds will continue fighting, but there will be more deaths, more sacrifices. ISIS, in his opinion, is worse than Saddam Hussein. As for why there are so many foreigners joining ISIS, he attributes it to being brainwashed.

Mr. JamaL Mutka

When I met with the senior commander of the Gwer forces, Mr. Jamal Mutka, he had just returned to his office, directly from the front lines. After updating me about the most recent attacks, I asked him what he believes ISIS's strategy is. Here's what he told me:

"ISIS wants full control of all of Iraq and Syria - to control all aspects of these areas, politically, religiously and economically. They want control of the entire world and they don't accept any beliefs others than their own. ISIS has goals outside of the region, but the first goal is to fully control Iraq and Syria and to have human power and the economics to influence the entire world."

I asked him to respond to US President Obama's comments that 99% of Muslims are peaceful. He responded that he doesn't agree with Obama - certain most Muslims desire peace, but not all. "Arab extremist don't accept any other beliefs. Maybe 60-70% are peaceful. But the remaining percentage are radical in some form."

On the topic of whether or not America is doing enough, he expressed appreciation for what America is currently offering. "But," he stated, "It is not enough considering the seriousness of the ISIS threat. We really want and need America's help. The U.S. is sending help to the Iraqi government but the flow of that help has been restricted due to economic issues. We need direct help and support."

He ended our conversation stating this: "Here's what I wish the Americans and the American government knew about the situation with ISIS and the efforts of the Kurds: The Kurds are peaceful, democratic, and have treated others fairly. We deserve American support in the war against ISIS and for our own recognized independence."

Everyday there are new stories of the violence and atrocities that ISIS is inflicting on humanity. Leaders of the world will have to decide how to effectively respond as lives hang in the balance. History is far too full of global action that showed up with too little, too late.

ISIS Advances: How Islamic is the Islamic State?

Phil Johnson, Ph.D.

From Erbil, Iraq

April 17, 2015

Today ISIS claimed responsibility for a car bombing near the U.S. consulate in Erbil, the capital of Iraqi Kurdistan. Yesterday, ISIS took over the eastern part of the city of Ramadi, in Iraq's Anbar province. Families with children could be seen carrying whatever they could, fleeing the city looking for safety in a very unsafe part of the world.

Reports of airstrikes from a U.S.-led coalition have helped to slow the advance, but the facts are that ISIS is not fading into the night – they continue to attract fighters from Arab and Western countries – and ISIS terrorists are definitely on the offensive.

One of the question that keeps coming up is this: "Is ISIS really Islamic or are they just a perversion of peaceful Islam?" A few weeks ago, I was in Iraq and sat down with two individuals to discuss this question. One is a journalist and former student of Islam, the other is an Imam and current Islamic scholar. Each had his on unique response to this question. Here is what they told me:

INTERVIEW WITH IBRAHIM HUSSEIN AHMED: JOURNALIST/FORMER STUDENT OF ISLAM (ERBIL, IRAQ)

Is Islam a peaceful religion?

"Your president Obama says that it is. But if Obama tells the truth that Islam is not a peaceful religion, he will engender outrage from much of the world. He can't tell the truth."

What about ISIS? Are they truly Islamic?

"ISIS came from Islam. There are rules in Islam that allow ISIS to do what they are doing. ISIS didn't come from another religion. There are contradictions in the Koran that create the problem. And ISIS takes advantage of these contradictions. Everyone can interpret as they want. In the history of Islam, what ISIS is doing now, they did this to Kurds – and they did it in the name of God, just as they are doing now. They think by doing these things, they will go to paradise.

"It says this in Islam. Most people don't have much information about the Koran. They think if it comes from God, it must be true and good.

"When you read the Koran carefully you end up with two choices, you either become like ISIS or you will become like a Communist— you believe all religions are lies. This was my journey as I studied Islam. I saw all the requirements, what Islam really said and what they really wanted from those who followed Islam. I just couldn't accept it."

So what is the real Islam?

"Most Muslims are confused about their beliefs and about what ISIS does. They need to read more. Ali, the son-in-law of the Prophet Muhammad, burned another Muslim when Ali became a Caliph. This is history. The Prophet Mohammad also burned Jews.

"ISIS takes advantage of the Koran, the Hadith or even fatwas (religious rulings). Maybe in the case of burning the Jordanian pilot, they just assumed a fatwa."

According to Ibrahim – it's not just his view of Islam that comes under scrutiny. According to him there are many conspiracy theories suggesting that the US and Britain are supporting ISIS. Recently supplies were delivered to ISIS, but from whom? Is the US bombing ISIS or supporting them? What would be the advantage to the U.S of supporting ISIS? "*Maybe*," according to Ibrahim, *"The U.S. wants to push the war away from themselves and let recruits for ISIS go to Iraq and die there. Or maybe it's just about creating a new map for the Middle East."*

INTERVIEW WITH IMAM SAFA GHANM ABDULLAH: ISLAMIC SCHOLAR/LEADER IN LOCAL MOSQUE (ERBIL, IRAQ)

Let's get right down to it: Is ISIS Islamic?
"They use the name. They use Islam. But what they are doing is not Islam."

Is Abu Bakr al Baghdadi, the leader of ISIS, qualified to lead a Caliphate?
"After Prophet Mohammed, there were four qualified leaders of a Caliphate. But after these four, no one is qualified unless there are elections."

Do you want there to be another Caliphate?
"We don't need this because we have the Koran and the Hadith and also the Prophet said, after me, there are only two things we need to follow, the Hadith and the Koran. We can use that to construct our daily lives."

What about the burning alive of the Jordanian pilot? What does the Koran say about that?
"Based on Islam, it is a peaceful religion. Even during wars and fights towards infidels, the Prophet told them not to kill the old or women, or children. Man is not to burn man, only God can do that."

If someone converts from Islam to another religion, should that be permitted? Or should the person who converts be killed by the official Islamic Sharia government.
"ISIS is a distortion of Islam – ISIS is distorting Islam and giving Islam a bad name. People are judging Muslims, even by their beards and they don't feel free. A legitimate Islamic state would be impossible, it's too hard to create this."

In January, eleven people who worked for the French satirical magazine *Charlie Hebdo* were murdered in Paris. The men responsible claimed their allegiance to al-Qaeda and ISIS. They justified their actions because the magazine published material insulting to Islam. How does Islam view free speech?
"There is freedom of speech in Islam. There are examples of free speech in Islamic history. But Muhammad is not alive – you cannot write or say anything bad about him. The people who created the insulting images of the Prophet should have been tried in a court."

In a court? Are you saying that the murderers should have been tried in court?
"No, the people who made the insulting comics should have been tried in court."

Why would there have been a trial for those using freedom of speech in a country such as France? What they were publishing wasn't illegal, even if that freedom offended others.
"It should have been left to the courts."

Then can you explain to me the difference between a Sharia government (where there is justification for cutting off hands, beheadings, stoning and the death penalty for leaving the Islamic faith) and what ISIS is doing?
"It's true about cutting off the hands. It is not practiced all the time – and should be done only by an Islamic state – by a legitimate Islamic state."

ISIS views themselves as a true, pure, accurate, legitimate Islamic state. What is the difference?
"I'm sorry, if you'll excuse me, it's time for prayers."

For the record, even with many follow-up questions, I could not get the Imam to say that murdering those who worked for the *Charlie Hebdo* magazine in Paris was wrong or an act of terror. Nor could I get him to clearly answer the question about the freedom of Muslims to convert to other religions or to clearly define the difference between ISIS and an Islamic Sharia government. Also for the record, I am not a proponent of purposefully offending others, but I am a proponent of freedom of thought, belief and expression.

These are just two of the conversations that I had in Iraq – I had many other off-the-record conversations. It always seems to come down to how the Koran is interpreted and contextualized. If you are a literalist, you might end up in the camp of ISIS. If you have a broader interpretation of the Koran and Islam, you will probably consider it as peaceful. But as several people told me during my visit, many simply don't know that much about what they believe or what the Koran says.

Finally: An Iran Nuke Deal

The "Great Satan" and the "World's Top Sponsor of Terrorism" Come to Terms

Phil Johnson, Ph.D.

July 15, 2015

From Frisco, Texas, USA

After years of talking about it, a deal was finally struck on Tuesday morning regarding Iran's nuclear program. As could be expected, not everyone agrees with it. The news of the deal struck some as the best thing ever, others felt it was the best that could be done under the circumstances, and others are calling it the worst deal in the history of bad deals. So let's take a look at what actually happened and what it might mean.

What the deal does:

In the briefest of explanations, the deal prevents Iran from getting a nuclear weapon - at least today. And probably for a decade. According to the deal:

1. Iran has to reduce its 19,000 centrifuges down to 6104 with only 5060 allowed to enrich uranium over the next 10 years.
2. Iran can only enrich uranium to 3.67% - not enough for a bomb.
3. Under the deal, Iran now faces a "one year break out period" to build a nuclear bomb. (Supposedly enough time to stop them if they start.)
4. Inspectors will have access to all declared nuclear facilities including Parchin, a military facility related to Iran's nuclear program.
5. Economic sanctions will be lifted by the international community (in time) as Iran proves that it has taken the key steps towards limiting its program. (That's going to be worth at least 150 billion dollars.)

So, if Iran plays it straight, their nuclear weapons program is kicked down the road a bit, but their nuclear program is certainly not dismantled - it's just sort of "paused."

What are critics really worried about:

While President Obama is celebrating his historic deal, there are many others who are not - especially the Republican Party and Israeli Prime Ministry, Netanyahu. President Obama, however, ensures that the agreement with Iran includes the most comprehensive inspection deal in history - and that it will provide more than enough evidence if Iran chooses to cheat. And then of course sanctions will be "snapped back" into place.

Some of the biggest concerns are:

1. The deal does nothing to change Iran's behavior in the Middle East.
2. In 5 years, conventional weapons can come into and out of Iran; In 8 years, ballistic missile can be bought and sold.
3. Iran will probably cheat on the deal - they do have a history of doing as they please.
4. The inspections give too much power in the hands of the Iranians being inspected. There are 24 day warnings before inspections, there can be challenges as to whether or not the inspections are warranted and military sites have the most protection from inspections.
5. Iran gets billions of dollars that have been previously held up in sanctions. What will they do with this money? Many believe that some of it will be used to continue the support of international terrorism - to organizations like Hamas and Hezbollah and the continued support of

Syria's president Assad.

6. It will be difficult to get current levels of sanctions back in place - China is itching to buy Iranian oil and Russia is salivating to start trading in conventional and ballistic weapons.

Does Iran Deserve to have a Nuclear Program, even if it Involves Weapons?

Eventually Iran will possess nuclear weapons. Maybe not today or tomorrow, but one day within the next decade, the game will change. Would that be the worst thing in the world? Other nations have achieved nuclear weapons and the world has gone on. Some, in fact believe that a nuclear armed Iran would actually bring stability to the region. Some believe that Israel's nuclear capability creates instability in the region and that another nuclear armed state would balance that power.

In 1964, after China became a nuclear power she became less volatile in her rhetoric. When India and Pakistan both became nuclear powers, they became more cautious. In the 70 years of the nuclear age, fears of rapid proliferation haven't really materialized. Not yet. But there's already street talk about Saudi trying to buy weapons from Pakistan, and talks going on in Turkey and Egypt about nuclear programs. So, time will tell.

Of course one valid concern is that Iran has actually suggesting using nuclear weapons against the US and Israel - and while some say that's just "political rhetoric," others do not dismiss the threats so easily. And even if Iran stops short of using a nuclear weapon, will having nukes embolden them in the region and increase their terrorist activities?

Is this the end of the world?

Well, it depends on who you talk to. Many religions have views of "the end of the world events" that often shape how they view the world, politics and current events.

With ISIS running rampant in Syria and Iraq and with Iran's new "nuke deal," you can expect lots of talk about the "apocalypse." ISIS believes they are living out the end days and are major players in Islamic prophecy. Iran's Shiite religious leaders are waiting for the appearance of al-Mahdi, a redeemer-like figure that will lead a great victory against Christians in a battle called al-Malhamah al-Kubrah or Armageddon. Some say al-Mahdi was never mentioned in the Koran, but that the Prophet Mohammed prophesied about him. Many Sunni Muslims believe that al-Mahdi hasn't been born yet.

On the Christian side, expect more chatter about prophecies in Ezekiel 37-39 where the Bible speaks about an alliance that forms between Turkey, Russia and Iran in the last days and instigate a major battle against Israel and ushers in another chapter of the end of the world as we know it.

There's nothing like the world of rocky geopolitical events to spark conversations about what's next, where the world is going and how it's all going to end. So I'll end this blog with a quote from Corrie ten Boom - a concentration camp survivor who knows all about an unstable world, *"If you look at the world, you'll be distressed. If you look within, you'll be depressed. If you look at God you'll be at rest."*

2015: The Last September?

Phil Johnson, Ph.D.
September 8, 2015
From Frisco, Texas, USA

Rarely has one single month received so much attention, or had some much going on! It does seem that this ninth month of the year has an unusually busy dance card - and most of it seems to hint at some grand ending for our planet. It's a feast for conspiracy theorists, but even if you're a skeptic, it's worth paying attention to the convergence of events happening in September 2015. Here's a brief rundown of some of the more significant events set to occur:

September 13: The last day of the Shemita year: So what's the deal with Shemita Years? It's the end of a cycle of seven years that's celebrated in Judaism. At the end of this period, farming land takes a rest and debts are cancelled. The last few Shemita years have brought huge financial challenges to the world. On September 17, 2001, just days after 9/11, the U.S. experienced a Wall Street crash. The next challenge was 7 years later on September 29, 2008 when the stock market crashed big time - again, on the last day of a Shemita year. And now here in September 2015, financial fears and rumblings are already beginning again. Some expect September 13th to be a troubling day for investments.

In addition, a leading authority in Ultra-Orthodox Judaism, Rabbi him Kanefsky, has been encouraging Jews to head to Israel in order to welcome the coming of the "messiah," which be believes will come at the end of the Sabbatical year - which is this September 13th.

September 15: UN Resolution of State of Palestine. It is possible that the UN could vote on making Palestine a recognized state during this 70th session of the UN General Assembly. According to the French plan, it would reinstate the pre-1967 boarders of Israel and split Jerusalem as the dual capital of both nations. At the moment, 136 nations have already recognized Palestine as a state, but the U.S. has always blocked recognition by the UN Security Council. Usually, when this vote comes up, it is vetoed by the U.S. But this time around - I'm not so sure that Obama will veto the measure. And if this measure is forced upon Israel without certain security preconditions being met - and if the city of Jerusalem is split, the end result will not be peace.

September 15: Jade Helm Exercises End: Officially, Jade Helm is a series of military exercises focusing on large scale irregular warfare. The exercises end September 15th. They are taking place in several Southern and Western States in the U.S. But there's something about large-scale military exercises, back helicopters and rumors of taking away the guns of citizens that brings out the most paranoid in citizens. Is Jade Helm just a way to prepare the U.S. army for special warfare elsewhere? Or are they planning a national takeover complete with martial law and detention centers? People aren't building compounds and stocking up on ammunition for fun!

September 17: Congress's last day to vote on Iran Deal: Love it or hate it - the world is making a deal with Iran that will release $150 billion that have been held up in sanctions and will pretty much pave the way for Iran to become a nuclear armed nation with all the weapons necessary to deliver its payload. While Congress fights each other about this issues and play with words like "treaty" and "constitutional authority," Iran is involved in a massive weapons shopping spree in Russia.

Most of the U.S. Congress - and U.S. citizens are against the deal. But President Obama will see that it goes through. Much of the rest of the world is OK with the deal - secret side deals and all. Saudi Arabia is not thrilled (whatever they may say in public) and Israel is definitely not happy about it. For Iran it's a total victory - and they are not ratcheting down their rhetoric against Israel or the U.S. in the slightest. The big question is, "Will Israel do something about it?" And if they do, how will the world respond? Israel has fewer friends than ever.

September 22/23: Day of Atonement: Yom Kippur, the Day of Atonement, is the holiest day on the Hebrew calendar. It begins at sunset September 22 and continues through sunset September 23. The Book of Daniel says that 49 years will follow the issuing of a command to restore Jerusalem until Messiah returns. He will "make atonement for iniquity" (Dan 9:24-25). September 23, 2015 will mark exactly 49 prophetic years (360 days each) since June 7, 1967, the day that a command to attack and conquer Jerusalem was given by the Israeli Minister of Defense, Moshe Dayan. Some Christians believe that the Rapture of the Church will happen on this day. (Leviticus 25:8-10 talks about sounding the loud trumpet throughout the land on this Day of Atonement.)

September 23/24: The Visit of the Pope to the US - Pope Francis will visit the U.S. - and apparently address Congress. He will be the first Pope to do so. Why? Most likely he will promote compassion towards immigrants, strengthening families, and battling inequality. I also understand that since it's a "holy year," it will be possible to absolve the sins of those who have had abortions - or at least the Pope is outsourcing it - allowing priests to offer the forgiveness for this sin, as long as the person is truly contrite. Hmmm - one last chance to get a few things right with God?

September 23/24: CERN (Center for European Nuclear Research) hits full power. Some in the scientific community have hinted that this might lead to the possibility of opening "parallel universes and extra dimensions."

September 23: **Eid-Ul-Adha Festival of Sacrifice**. As if September 23 was not busy enough, this dates marks, for Muslims, the willingness for Abraham to almost sacrifice his son Ishmael. This festival also marks the end of the Hajj pilgrimage to Mecca.

September 28: The Blood Moons coinciding with Jewish feast days. 2014-2015 have brought the rare tetrad (4 in-arow) lunar eclipses called "Blood Moons." Each of the four has fallen exactly on a significant Jewish feast day. Some are connecting these events to what the Bible says about the moon turning to blood in the last days. (Joel 2:30-31 and Revelation 6:12) The final blood moon is scheduled to appear on September 28, the Jewish Feast of the Tabernacle. Some are predicting anything from world-wide earthquakes to the return of Jesus.

Additional intriguing tidbits:

Human history is about to celebrate its 6000th birthday? For those who hold to a "young earth" theory - human history is approaching its 6000th birthday. Starting with Adam and following the subsequent genealogies as listed in the Bible, the earth is about 6000 years old.

One of the reasons, say supporters, that this is significant is that 6000 years equal 120 jubilee cycles (49 years, plus one), lending itself to Genesis 6:3 where God says, "My Spirit will not contend with humans forever for they are mortal; their days will be a hundred twenty years." Could it be that God was speaking about 120 cycles of Jubilees? 120 x 50 years = 6000 years?

If this intrigues you, check out www.torahcalendar.com - an interesting resource combining ancient historical records,

Scripture, and advanced knowledge of lunar and planetary motions. The owners say they've got the exact dates all sorted out. Using a 360-day lunar calendar (rather that than today's Gregorian Calendar) these fellows think they've got the dates all figured out. Why does it matter? Because it makes sense that God would mirror creation in six days followed by one day of rest and then allow human history to drag on for 6000 years, follow by a period of judgment and 1000 years of a millennium. Tick tock, tick tock…

Several Imams are expecting the coming of the Madhi Coming in September? It's not just the Jews and Christians who are predicting "apocalyptical" events in the near future. According to some Imams, September is the month for the coming of the Mahdi - the redeemer-like figure that has been waiting for the right moment - who will appear only when the world is pushed towards chaos and degradation. He will appear and help lead humanity to a pan-Islamic world.

Well, that should be enough to keep you on your toes during the month of September. If it turns out to be true - and if the world is entering a brand new phase, if financial disaster will befall all of us, if the Christian church will be raptured out of the Earth while God delivers divine punishment, if the the Mahdi appears and takes over the world, all I've got to say is this: be sure of what you believe - the future is not something to gamble with.

"Watch ye therefore, and pray always, that ye may be accounted worthy to escape all these things that shall come to pass, and to stand before the Son of man." Luke 21:36

A Lingering September 2015

A Middle East View of Where the World is Headed

Phil Johnson, Ph.D.

September 25, 2015

From Cairo, Egypt

As the month of September drags on, people are still waiting for a number of apocalyptic episodes to take place. Personally, I've been waiting to see if I should pay my mortgage for October or not, while waiting for Palestine to become a state, looking for blood moons to appear and watching for Jesus or the Mahadi to make a personal appearance. But while doing all of that, I decided to keep myself busy chasing global stories and investing in young leaders in the Middle East, specifically in Egypt and Iraq over the last two weeks.

While speaking at a conference this month in Cairo, Egypt, I decided to find out what my students really thought about some current global events. The group of students are predominantly university students and young business professionals. The majority of them are Muslim, with a small minority being Christian. The goal was to find out what others, (these students) living in a vastly different part of the world (compared to the U.S.) thought about current world issues. Here are some of their thoughts:

What was your reaction to the beheading of 21 Coptic Christians, lined up in orange jumpsuits, by ISIS in Libya (February 2015).

All respondents believed this episode was a horrible, unbelievable event. Some interjected a political aspect and propaganda into how ISIS orchestrated the event, and almost all stated that this act had nothing to do with the tenants of the Islamic faith.

- Noha said, *"I'm totally against what happened. It's a shame that it's under the name of Islam..."*

- *Ahmed said, "It was a disaster. It was for media purposes to sell the world on the idea of ISIS."*

- Nada said, "*I think it is a very aggressive group and they deserve to all be killed because they sparked fear all over the world.*"

- *Mohamed Islam believed, "I think it was an edited video that ISIS wanted to use to frighten people, but overall I was upset at their violence against people whatever their religious direction."*

- *Mohamad Mamdouh expressed that he wanted to take action against such a situation, but "like many others, I had nothing to do but watch and share my thoughts on Facebook."*

- *An unnamed respondent stated this, "It changed my idea about ISIS. Because for a while there I thought they would be something good. Then I see them killing people whether these people are wrong or right. They don't have the right to decide to end lives like that."*

ISIS, or the Islamic State, is the first terrorist organization to control their own Caliphate since the Ottoman Empire. They are also infamous for their horrific acts of brutality towards some Muslim groups, Christians and other minorities. How would you describe ISIS (The Islamic State in Iraq and Syria) as an organization?

- 89% of those who responded viewed ISIS as simply not Islamic at all- that the behaviors and goals of ISIS have nothing to do with their own understanding of Islam and how it should be practiced.

- About 10% believed that ISIS is in fact Islamic- but a radical form and radical interpretation of the religion.

- Ahmed (whose view represented less than 1% of those surveyed) viewed the whole affair as a political form of Islam designed to serve the Super Powers in the Middle East.

Do you think the recent nuclear deal with Iran is a good thing for the world, and in particular, for Egypt and the region? Are you comfortable with Iran increasing their influence in the region?

The overall feelings of the Egyptians we interviewed was that it was a bad idea for Iran to procure nuclear weapons. In fact, 95% were clearly against it while 5% either didn't feel they had enough information to comment or that there were some pros and cons to Iran's nuclear ambitions.

- *Passant Abn El Moniem refuses the idea of the "existence of nuclear weapons in the world."*

- *Mohamed Islam echoed this concerns stating that eventually "nuclear weapons would destroy the world."*

- *Basem Moataz believes that the Iran Deal will trigger a nuclear arms race in the Middle East, and says, "I don't think we are ready for that."*

End of the world: There is much talk lately about the imminent end of the world. How do you think the world is going to end? Do you think it will happen in your lifetime?

There has been so much talk recently, especially regarding the month of September 2015, that many signs, prophetic and otherwise, are lining up and indicating that the world is about to see its final days. We wanted to know if this group of Egyptians we were working with had the same sense that things were winding down. (After all, both Christianity and Islam have prophecies and views of the end of the world.)

Nearly all of the respondents believed that the world was going to end - that we were headed toward nuclear disaster, some cosmic disturbance or the destruction of our planet due to poor resource management. A few believe that prophetic signs pointed towards the near end of the world.

Overall, a little less than half of those surveyed thought that they might witness Earth's last days. The slight majority either didn't know, didn't think think anyone could know, or they simply believed that while things were getting bad, the world would continue to turn and churn out iPhones and other essential gadgets. Here are some of the individual comments:

- *Saga said, "The selfishness is increasing, with everyone caring only about their own selves even at the expense of others..."*

- *Mostafa El-Tabey says, "I don't know and I don't expect anything. God only knows."*

- Mohab Farid says, *"The world is going to end, due to the death of the planet, due to excessive use of its resources. It won't happen in my lifetime, but in the next 100 to 200 years."*

- Hadeer Hatem says, *"I have no idea how it is going to end, but what's scary is that it was stated in our religion that certain small and big signs would appear, then the day of justice would come and the world would come to an end. Most of the small signs have come true, so based on our religion, this means that the end of the world is getting closer..."*

Currently, many refugees are flowing into Europe from Syria, Iraq, Afghanistan and many other places experiencing conflict. Experts are saying this is the largest mass movement of refugees into Europe since World War II. Reports are saying that many are converting to Christianity as they enter these Western nations. What do you think of this? Are these real conversions? Are these "conversions" for political reasons? For some other reason?

There are reports that many refugees are converting from Islam to Christianity - and while some reports coming out of nations like Germany indicated that the conversions seem genuine, there is, of course the possibility that some are converting to increase their chances of gaining asylum in their new country. (No European country forces or encourages conversion, but someone who converts could say that as a new convert, he or she would face persecution or death if returned to their former Muslim country.)

I thought it would be interesting to ask these Egyptian students - most of whom are Muslims, what they thought about the conversions of these refugees - were they genuine or fake? Most of the responses indicated doubt that the conversations were real. Some felt that the refugees were confused, had shallow faith, or felt pressured to convert to have a better chance of gaining asylum. Unsurprisingly, there was not a lot of support for the ideas that the Holy Spirit was working in the hearts and lives of men and women who had been through horrific times and were embracing the grace, forgiveness and the love of Jesus. Here is a sampling of their responses:

- Pasant Abd El Moniem, *"I think it is only conversion for political reasons."*

- Nada Hatem Shaheen, *"I don't think the conversions are real and if it happens, it will be public only, but for themselves, they will still remain in their former religion."*

- Hammam, *"I don't think this is true, it may be fake conversions just to guarantee to stay safe in their new countries..."*

- Maryam Ahmad, *"I think this is sad. Even if people decided to convert to Christianity, finding a more embracing religion, this should not at all be connected to them being refugees. No one should be forced to changed his beliefs in order to survive."*

- Mohab Farid, *"I am not sure it these are real conversions, but it might be a play from the refugees or the media to get the people's sympathies."*

- Hadeer Hatem, *"I think theses conversions are for political reasons, so that they feel safer and more secure if they are not considered Muslims."*

- Rana Younes Badr, *"Assuming that this is true, for a part, I can't blame them because they really suffered and the people who did this to them are Muslims or maybe it's more accurate to say "fake Muslims."*

Whether or not the world ends this month - as so many have predicted - and whether or not the Mahdi makes his appearance or Jesus returns or if World War IIII breaks out - one thing is for certain, the world continues to change, violence is increasing, desperation is growing and it appears deception (on a personal level and global level) is at an all-time high. There are always turning points in history - always moments that change the course of things and the nature of our world. And at difficult times like these, there are also people who step up to make a difference in this world. I hope we all will be these types of people.

BIBLIOGRAPHY
THE SOURCES

BIBLIOGRAPHY

The sources

Basco, Monica Ramirez, Ph.D. The Procrastinator's Guide to Getting Things Done. New York: Guilford Press, 2010.

Belsky, Scott. Making Ideas Happen: Overcoming the obstacles between vision and reality. New York: the Penguin Group, 2010.

Bethge, Eberhard. Dietrich Bonhoeffer: A Biography. Augsburg Fortress Publishers, 2000.

Chabris, Christopher and Simons, Daniel. The Invisible Gorilla: And other ways our intuitions deceive us. New York: Crown, 2010.

Cohen, David Elliot. What Matters: The world's preeminent photojournalists and thinkers depict essential issues of our time. New York: Sterling Publishing, 2008.

Gladwell, Malcolm. The Tipping Point: How little things can make a dig difference. New York: Little Brown and Company, 2002.

Haidt, Jonathan. The Happiness Hypothesis: Finding modern truth in ancient wisdom. New York: Basic Books, 2006.

Harris, Alex and Brett. Do Hard Things: A teenage rebellion against low expectations. Colorado Springs, CO: Multnomah Books, 2008.

Harris, Alex and Brett. Start Here: Doing hard things right where you are. Colorado Springs, CO: Multnomah Books, 2010.

Heath, Chip and Heath, Dan. Switch: How to change things when change is hard. New York: Broadway Books, 2010.

Hofstede, Geert. (2003) *Cultural Dimensions.* http://health.msn.com/health-topics/slideshow.aspx?cp-documentid=100252883

Iyengar, Sheena, The Art of Choosing. New York: Twelve Hachette Book Group, 2010.

Jeremiah, David. Slaying the Giants in Your Life. Nashville: W Publishing Group, 2001.

Maloof, Rich. 2010. "Top Phobias of 2010" *MSN: Health and Fitness.* http://health.msn.com/health-topics/slideshow.aspx?cp-documentid=100252883

Marano, Hara Estroff. "Procrastination: "Ten Things to Know" *Psychology Today*. August 23, 2003. http://www.psychologytoday.com/articles/200308/procrastination-ten-things-know

Miller, Donald. A Million Miles in a Thousand Years: What I learned while editing my life. Nashville, Thomas Nelson, 2010.

Peters, Tom. The Little Big Things: 163 ways to pursue excellent. Harper Collins, 2010.

Pink, Daniel. Drive: The surprising truth about what motivates us. New York: Riverhead Books, 2009.

Strickler, Jane. (2006) "What Really Motivates People?" *Journal for Quality and Participation.* http://findarticles.com/p/articles/mi_qa3616/is_200604/ai_n17172791/

Shapira, Oren, Liberman, Nira. "An Easy Way to Increase Creativity" *Scientific American.* July 21, 2009. http://www.scientificamerican.com/article.cfm?id=an-easy-way-to-increase-c&page=2

Ten Boom, Corrie. The Hiding Place. Grand Rapids, MI: Chosen Books, 1971, 1984.

Thomson, Gale. "David Livingstone," *Encyclopedia of World Biographies.* 2006. http://findarticles.com/p/articles/mi_qa3616/is_200604/ai_n17172791/

Weingarten, Gene. (2007) "Pearls Before Breakfast," *The Washington Post*, http://www.washingtonpost.com/wp-dyn/content/article/2007/04/04/AR2007040401721.html

Made in the USA
Columbia, SC
20 March 2020